Speak Up!

Speak Up!

A Woman's Guide to Presenting Like a Pro

Cyndi Maxey, CSP

AND

Kevin E. O'Connor, CSP

St. Martin's Griffin
New York

SPEAK UP! Copyright © 2008 by Cyndi Maxey and Kevin E. O'Connor. All rights reserved. Printed in the United States of America. For information, address St. Martin's Press, 175 Fifth Avenue, New York, N.Y. 10010.

www.stmartins.com

Library of Congress Cataloging-in-Publication Data

Maxey, Cyndi.
    Speak up! : a woman's guide to presenting like a pro / Cyndi Maxey and Kevin E. O'Connor.—1st ed.
        p. cm.
    ISBN-13: 978-0-312-37628-4
    ISBN-10: 0-312-37628-6
    1. Public speaking for women.   I. O'Connor, Kevin E.   II. Title.
    PN4192.W65M39 2008
    808.5'1082—dc22

                                                                    2008023606

First Edition: November 2008

10   9   8   7   6   5   4   3   2   1

For my daughter Phelan Elizabeth, who is beautiful inside and out, and my son Ryan Kenneth, who is athletic and artistic energy personified. May they both learn and live the benefits of Speaking Up!

—Cyndi Maxey

For Dr. Barbara Myers, a friend and an encourager who taught me to Speak Up while she said I was teaching her. Maybe that is the way it is supposed to work anyway!

—Kevin E. O'Connor

Contents

Acknowledgments

We begin by thanking all those who read our first collaboration, *Present Like a Pro: The Field Guide to Mastering the Art of Business, Professional, and Public Speaking* (St. Martin's Press, 2006), giving it the vote of confidence that inspired the beginnings of this book. Thank you to our editors at St. Martin's Press—Sheila Curry-Oakes and Alyse Diamond—for their inspiration, detailed yet big-picture minds, and, yes, womanhood! We give special thanks to our agent, Jay Poynor—who has our undying admiration for the years of savvy relationship-building that led us to St. Martin's Press.

We thank all the great women and men quoted herein who spoke up—sharing their time and wise stories. Their candor and professionalism anchored our concepts with real-life lessons: our gratitude to Judy Schueler; Angela Ray, PhD; Adrienne Antink, CAE; Amy Huntington; Anita Blanchard, MD; Maria Pappas, JD, PhD; Lisa Monde, Kristin MacGregor; Diane Kubal; Mary Lynn Fayoumi; Deborah Lee, MD, PhD; Mary Krueger; Karen Deis; Nanne Finis; Bill Kurtis; Anne Eiting Klamar, MD; Carolyn Smeltzer, RN, EdD; Michelle Gadsden-Williams; Helen Torley, MD; Jill Berry Bowen, RN, CHE; Gail Wolf; Jeri Stewart, RN; Marie-Chantal Simard, PhD; Tammy Bratton, PharmD; Jane Jackson Esparza; Elizabeth Wailes; Susan LaVenture; Erin McKinney, JD; Julie Kaiser; Joan Sparks; and Shawn Tomasello. We also thank Fran Vlasses, RN, PhD; Ling Wu, MD; Greg Kozar;

Sue Truman; Darryl Rosen; and Rob Brenner, MD, who helped us locate these contributors. And we thank our encouraging friends, clients, mentors, and coaches, Ken Johnson, PharmD; Tim McNamara, PharmD; Todd Yancey, MD; Ken Massey, PharmD; and Nido Qubein.

We thank our families for listening, tolerating, supporting, and cheering us on as we completed this second book together—not always an easy feat! Cyndi thanks Rob, Ryan, and Phelan Maxey, as well as her dad, Ken Adcock, and her brother's family: Therry, Jill, Rilla, and Leon Adcock. Kevin thanks Rita for allowing him all that time writing while she studied, Corbb, an early editor and constructive critic, and Lanty, who labored over the final copy, making it much easier on the writer!

Foreword

A man presents, a woman presents. Who has more credibility?

We want to say that the presenter who knows more, prepares better, and communicates most effectively wins, but our experience shows that, over and over again, the man wins hands down. And, believe it or not, women are the ones who tell us this!

That isn't fair and it isn't right; it may not even be true. However, if women believe that it's true, if their experience says that is the case, and if others reinforce it, how might that affect their performance, their influence, even their next speech? How would it affect *your* next presentation?

As career-long speakers and speaker coaches, we have seen the effects of female influence or lack of it. We have coached, observed, and counseled hundreds of women who are smart, motivated, unique, and inspired—but are unable to convey those attributes when they most want and need to do so. We write this book to encourage and inspire you to be *you*—the wonderful, talented woman that you are. We bring our male and female viewpoints to provide you with an honest, non-gender-biased perspective. In fact, we carefully coauthored each and every chapter and had many illuminating discussions in the process!

Why are effective speaking and presenting skills so important for women? They convey the essence of you—your talents, your history, and your personality—in a short amount of time. They anchor decisions that are being made about you, whether you know it or not. They determine if you will influence the outcome of important decisions that will affect many. Whether you present one-on-one, to small groups, or to larger audiences, your ability to convey your ideas is tantamount to your career success.

The following chapters have been carefully chosen to give you our essential message: When you, the female presenter, find your authentic voice and a way to deliver its power, it will dramatically impact your career, your life, and the way you think about yourself. As a result of reading this book, you will speak up with conviction and clarity. You will never underestimate your ability to present your ideas to another person or group when faced with the opportunity. You will develop your natural strengths and work positively with feedback in order to get the results you want from your next presentation.

The chapters that follow are short and to the point. We want them to be inspiration for you, not an academic discourse. We want you to read and react, adapt and experiment. We want to be your trusted coaches in print, if not in person. Great coaches help you stretch, take risks, think, and rethink. Great coaches think ahead of those they coach, and so we want to give you a heads-up in all those areas of presenting with which you may be unfamiliar. We want you to walk on the playing field at the top of your game.

While we are fully supportive of what you do, we also want to challenge you, because for the most part, today's business world is still discriminatory and unfair to women. Women's ideas are often taken less seriously than those of their male peers; women hold fewer roles of authority; women take on "details work" while others get the "big-picture projects."

But this need not be the case for you.

Simply put, if you can present well, others will think of you as a capable, articulate individual. The ability to speak, present, and facilitate groups is the number one skill for women in business today. You may find that as a woman you sometimes struggle to be heard, and for that reason it is vital for you to find and use your female voice most effectively and with utmost clarity. We are here to help you speak up and be heard, from the boss's office to the conference room.

She was so knowledgeable of her subject and organized in her thoughts that she did not need to refer to any notes, and spoke directly to the audience by telling stories that tied in with her message. The way that she described the stories and tied her message together was so captivating and inspiring. She had the entire audience at the edge of their seats and received a standing ovation.

Susan LaVenture
Executive Director
National Association for Parents of
Children with Visual Impairments

Introduction

Why would women need a special book on presentation skills? If you're a woman reading this, you may be thinking, *Okay, I'll take a look, but what will they tell me that they wouldn't tell a man?* That is a very good question. Our goal is for you to see that the question is not "Why?" but rather "Why not?" or even "Why not sooner?"

Women *Are* Different!

In our years working with talented professionals of all genders in a multitude of organizations and situations, it became clear to us that women encounter special challenges in the workplace. More is expected of them today, they are evaluated more judgmentally, and they have to work harder than their male counterparts for equal treatment, respect, and influence. Women do things differently—they think differently and they react differently. We know that women understand their emotions more deeply and express them more overtly than men do. Why do women tend to gather substantial and diverse information rather than laser in on one specific issue? Why do women talk more softly and use less assertive language than men? All the well-documented communication differences that apply to women in general also apply to women as presenters and influencers, with one exception—the women who know the secret to getting their point across are a breed apart.

Women *Are* Determined!

Are you determined to become more poised and effective in front of a group? Do you want to learn, once and for all, how to present your ideas to a boss? Is discovering how to be heard in a team meeting important to you? This book is designed to help you succeed in three key areas to meet those goals by giving you the following tools: (1) preparation steps to set you up for success, (2) presentation skills to boost your impact, and (3) tried and true techniques for maintaining professionalism, which will give you the edge.

The Three P's:
Preparation, Presentation,
and Professionalism

Preparation, Presentation, and Professionalism—if you stretch yourself in all three areas, you experience a true ProStretch. That's our challenge to you as you consider new ideas. View us as your personal trainers urging you on with this book as your workout guide. We want you to "go for the burn," as trainers often urge—that point where you know you've done something new and different and you can "feel" it. We want this book to be a ProStretch for women and others at work, women at home leading groups, women in school, and young women new on the job. After reading this book, you will know how to harness your voice and excel in any speaking situation, from conference rooms to the annual conference.

The women who succeed in speaking situations have taken stock of their audience and know how to respond to the different personalities in the room. They know who will support them and who will challenge them, and are prepared to respond effectively and professionally.

Present to Influence

Women tend to fall into presentation traps of apology, self-deprecation, self-doubting, minimizing achievement, using tentative language, and getting lost in detail—to name just a few. They need to learn opposite behaviors: communicating self-assuredness, maximizing achievements, speaking with certainty, and being clear about the ROI (return on investment) and the end game (results) of everything they present. In this book, you will learn to harness what every great female is in touch with—the voice within yourself.

The Outcome Belongs to You

One mistake women make is to continue their old patterns of hoping that "next" time will be "the" time they'll get it right. That is dangerous thinking. Many women follow the dictum, "If you always do what you always did, you'll always get what you've always got," and that will not help you to break yourself of old habits. Choose instead to be innovative, change in important ways, and apply our tips and inside information in order to skyrocket your career and your life goals. Join us—we're there with you every step of the way.

> *Poise is a big deal. If you are not poised, you will not be seen as in charge and in command and are going to have a tough time winning trust and belief in your messages. A great woman I recently hired, who I thought was too young and inexperienced for the level job for which she was interviewing, blew me away*

with the poise and precision in the way she presented herself. She had instant credibility because of the confidence that she displayed, and this gave her a decided advantage over her male counterparts, winning her the job.

Tim McNamara, PharmD
Vice President, Clinical Research and Medical Affairs
ISTA Pharmaceuticals
Irvine, CA

PART 1

Present to Impress

1

Be Major When You're the Minority

Most women in business will have to face the time when she is the only woman in the room. When you're in the gender minority, be grateful rather than fearful. Accept that you will have some challenges but know that you also will have some advantages. You'll stand out, so men will be naturally curious: How did you get there? What are you like? Are you "one of the guys"? What do you know that they don't know? You have the power to turn that curiosity into genuine interest. How? Because you're a woman, you'll observe and listen more readily to the nuances of the situation: Who sits first? Who laughs loudest? Why are some people still on their cell phones? Who has the most paperwork? Who asked to help? You can use those observations to make decisions on how to lead and participate. Women add a new dynamic to business communication.

Whether you're at a small team project meeting or a larger event, now is your opportunity to shine. Never underestimate the career-building potential of your presence at meetings, even seemingly mundane regular meetings. We've heard top executives discuss individuals after a meeting—they don't miss a thing. Consider everything you say an opportunity to make a powerful impression.

Be Certain Like a Man

We have heard women at every level, from assistant to executive, speak in ways that lack steadfastness and undermine their confidence and authority. Have you ever caught yourself saying

"We kind of need to get going on this project."

"There are, like, too many, y'know, of these on the front burner."

"How would you sort of like to proceed?"

"I really don't think this will get us where we were trying to be."

Now, imagine the difference when you speak with confidence and authority:

"We need to move on this now."

"We have to make a priority decision."

"What do you want to do next?"

"This won't work."

In order to be taken seriously, think before you speak, and speak with certainty. *Like, umm, kind of,* and *sort of* scream insecurity, not influence.

The Devil Is in the Details

Don't get lost in the process of gathering details when you are the only female in the group. Be able to pull up detail when needed, but only when the time is right. Men tend to think in bigger pictures and toward one target. There will come a point when they will need your "on tangent" perspective to their "on target" shooting. But wait until the right time.

Our goal is to help you understand how to be most effective when presenting to men. Men—especially skeptical men—respond best to facts and data. When you present the facts and data in the context of a problem or an issue that is important to them, they will pay attention. It shows them that you are well prepared, that you are a force to be reckoned with, and that you are thinking "like a man" about the topic. Facts and data are to a man what Tinkertoys are to a boy, what engine parts are to a racecar driver. You simply can't build without them.

Inspire with Mental Pictures

Begin with facts and data, but take that one step further and carefully engage your audience by using metaphors, mental pictures, and thoughtful images to piece the message together. For example, a new sales strategy could be described as a six-step "workout"; customer focus might be visualized with digital photos; a new benefits plan could be analogous to maintaining a healthy environment or lawn. It's a step that men often overlook in their own presentations but one they will appreciate in yours. If you want to be truly successful, know your data cold and win over the experts by throwing in some interesting trivia-like tidbits to show that you've done your research but that you're not just there to present the facts. Examples might include when the product you are presenting was invented and by whom, how it got its name, and any other little-known facts that will interest your audience, especially the men in the room.

Since sports and TV are a major source of entertainment for a lot of men, those references will work well in your presentations to a male audience. Your goal here is twofold: to encourage your audience and also to be memorable when you leave. With a little extra thought, you can easily build in sports references. Read the sports section the day of your presentation and be able to refer to a local team. If you play tennis, relate the challenge of playing at the net to nearing a

sales close. If you hike or jog, convey the sensation of adrena-
line flowing to a step in the change process. The same is true
for television references: Check out your media news source
for new, popular shows or talk show gossip. Be able to toss
out the name of a TV celebrity that is appropriate to the age
group you're addressing. Often these references lighten the
tone of the presentation and contribute to rapport building.

The Task at Hand

When you are ready to ask for agreement or action from
your male audience, use phrases like the following: you may
want to consider, the reason this is important is because, others have thought, an important benefit is . . . These are all
ways to gently guide action without sounding too brash or
forceful.

What do men want from a female presenter? Most men
want to hear a competent speaker who has a friendly and
engaging persona, is a nonthreatening encourager to action,
and a helpful commander of the essentials of what the audience needs to know now. In short, men want from a woman
what they appreciate from a man—a nonthreatening equal
up to the task at hand. The same applies when speaking to
your male boss one on one as it does for larger groups. He's
looking forward to your authentic self as well as your ac-
tionable ideas.

Discounted Female Need Not Be

Female managers repeatedly complain that their actions are
misinterpreted or discounted. When they know the group
needs to get busy with work, they are seen as controllers,
yet when they have every detail accounted for, they are criticized for not understanding the big picture. Men, on the

other hand, are rewarded for "seeing the big picture" rather than "delving into the detail." Male executives can make demands and not be seen as control freaks. Women are confused by what they see as a double standard. The bottom line is that men are rewarded on a *different* standard.

Male executives know the rules that have been laid out by years and generations of other male executives. Getting the job done is preferred to getting it done "just right." Attending to the important details is preferred to attending to "every" detail. The male executives we work with tell us that making decisions without having all the facts is commonplace for them. Saying something important in passing is preferred to saying something and documenting it in triplicate.

Additionally, men have become accustomed to women serving them at the workplace. At your office, who cleans up the coffee room? Who is the one appointed to be the "secretary" for some small group processes? What is the gender of most of the administrative coordinators at your office? How are they complimented and spoken of? How do they see their jobs? And who is the one who is the brunt of most of the gender-related jokes? Knowing the answers to these questions (and there are many different answers) need not make us resentful or boastful, only wiser about those we present to and those we present for.

Know the Rules to Break Them

When you know the rules, then you can play by them. When you really understand them, you can influence them. And when you know the rules very, very well, you can break them.

The female executive presenter must operate from knowledge and not resentment, from wisdom and not a blind obedience to the culture, from today's values and not from an antiquated idea of what she thinks is needed. She must operate from efficiency and not perfection. What she was taught as a young girl about service and femininity must be replaced with a new definition of both.

When she operates in a male environment, she need not "put up" with lesser status, she needs only to understand and operate in the understanding of what makes others successful, what moves a team forward, and what the real need is in each and every individual present. The days of women trying to act and be like men are on their way out. The best female presenters understand that the best presentation is one that allows them to be seen as a woman who knows that "one extra thing" very well. That "one extra thing" she has gained through acute perception of the audience's needs—whether it be affirmation, acknowledgment, or intense data on key issues. She can verbalize it for them and extract it from them simultaneously.

> **With a male audience,**
>
> - You don't need to become "one of the *guys*." Don't make the mistake of some female comedians and many executives by assuming more "male" characteristics of dress, language, and humor. Consider who you are at your female essence. Some of you are tough, no-nonsense individuals. Some are demure and quiet. Others are introspective. Be yourself, stay on message, and remain confident in your unique way, without resorting to acting more masculine. When you try to be more "like them," you run the risk of minimizing who you are.
>
> - Know their issues. Be ready to articulate the issues well. If you have the time and access to your audience, conduct brief phone interviews prior to your presentation. These

prepresentation interviews will help you greatly. You might even reference them in your presentation for greater credibility. Ask your interviewees if you can quote them by name. The more people you enlist on your side, the better they will understand the point you are making.

- Liberally affirm the general intention of the audience or the initiative. While not a strictly female trait, affirmation comes across with more aplomb from a female presenter. It may sound like the following: "While this is a difficult time we're going through, it's clear that this team has the right attitude. I can see it in your reactions to the data today and I hear it in your project reports." Or it may simply be, "Thank you for all you do for the IT department; it is appreciated, even on the darkest of days." Affirmation must not seem in any way sarcastic or to be any form of a put-down. It must be seen as genuine. In fact, this technique is a very good one to get a hostile audience on your side. Few of us dislike affirmation.

Women, when speaking today, often prepare more thoroughly, and think more self-consciously about personal appearance, because they feel the pressure to demonstrate their competence. For example, when I started teaching, I put on a suit every day to help create a sense of authority. Many students expect women instructors to be warm, nurturing, and kind, but credibility and knowledge are not automatically assumed.

Angela G. Ray, PhD
Assistant Professor of Communication
   Studies
Northwestern University
Evanston, Illinois

2

Find Your Female Voice

The female voice can be one of the most persuasive instruments on the planet—or it can be one of the most grating and distracting. We'd like you to think of your natural voice as a precious and beautiful trait. In essence, every woman's natural voice is beautiful; it just gets corroded with bad habits along the way. Those habits may include inadequate breathing, poor use of the vocal apparatus (lips, tongue, teeth), ineffective pitch and tone, or lazy projection of volume, to name a few. Poor habits are often heightened when presenting.

Have you ever left your boss's office embarrassed by the high-pitched squeaks you heard come out of your mouth during your project update? You knew you were a bit nervous, but you sounded like Minnie Mouse! Awareness is the first step to finding your voice. Now you need to do something about it. If you are like many of the women we coach, you will find it helpful to record your voice in order to hear subtle changes caused by emotions, the time of day, what you wear, and your level of stress. By recording your voice, you will pick up on the vocal habits you have perpetuated, without even realizing it. Record yourself often at various events and times of day. Recording your end of the conversation on your phone is also helpful; you'll hear how your voice sounds to others. Make a note of the fit of the clothing and shoes you are wearing: clothing can constrict you if it is tight or uncomfortable; shoes, especially heels, can make a difference in your overall ability to breathe and project sound because they affect your posture and muscle tension.

We watched a female executive respond to a question while seated among a group of colleagues. Her voice was muffled and slight, and we had a hard time hearing her, so we asked her to stand up and speak more loudly from her place among the group. When she stood, a remarkable thing happened. Her voice changed. It was clear, commanding, solid, and easy to understand throughout the room. Believe it or not, she was unaware of how powerful her voice became when she stood up to speak. From that point forward, we asked her to use her "standing voice" even when she was sitting down. She came to appreciate what that meant. She became aware of her "standing voice" and was able to be a full participant and leader in the group.

If volume is an issue for you (as it is for many female speakers who speak softly), chances are you are not breathing correctly. Breath should be supported by the diaphragm to boost your volume level; volume in front of a group needs to be louder than one on one. Many women simply speak at the same level in front as they do sitting down. When you're standing, take deep breaths, expanding your abdominal and chest area, and push the sound out! Make this a habit every time you stand to present for a team meeting, a board presentation, or a product review—even for five or six audience members. If most of your presentations are one to one, be very aware of sitting tall so that you have room to breathe.

For larger groups, make the microphone your friend. You definitely need a microphone for groups of fifty or more; most business environments designed for fifty or more are also designed for audiovisual equipment. One of our favorites is the cordless lavaliere mike (a small mike that is attached to you with a clip) because it allows you to move around. A lavaliere mike, when clipped securely about three to four inches from your mouth, is an invaluable ally. In general, ask trusted colleagues if they can hear you; encourage them to tell you the truth. If you can't be heard, nothing else matters. Worse, you've made yourself an example of a female stereotype—the soft-spoken, unassertive type.

It is crucial to identify how others perceive your voice, especially when you are presenting to men who pride themselves on having strong voices that fill a room. Women's voices vary more widely in pitch and tone. Some have a deep, husky sound, while others rely on a cute voice that is perky and lively. Still others have an interesting accent or twang they have owned from day one. Each voice has its own character and its own purpose. Our job here is not to tell you to eliminate your vocal style, but to suggest that you become keenly aware of it. Awareness is the key and a powerful skill for anyone who wants to influence—one on one or before a group.

Always speak with more volume and energy than you will in a one-on-one conversation. If a microphone is present, use it. Never ask, "Can you hear me without the mike?" because nobody will tell you the truth. If your audience is largely baby boomers and older, chances are that a percentage will have some form of undiagnosed hearing problem. Always take command and use the mike that's there. Even for a small group, a good 20 percent will be happy you used it. They might not even be aware of their hearing problem, but they will be happy to have heard you loud and clear. That is the point.

Speak into the mike with a natural volume. Be careful that you don't raise your pitch. By raising the pitch of your voice, you will be more likely to squeak. This squeak under stress most often happens if you are excited or nervous. You have quite a range of pitch levels in your natural voice. To find them, try counting from one to ten, starting as low-pitched as you can and getting very high-pitched by the number ten. (The sound at the ten-count is how you might sound if you were sunburned.) Be aware of this range, and when you're tense in front of a group, take a deep breath and mentally remind yourself to pitch your voice in the lower range. Pause and breathe to keep the pitch placed where you want it. Again, taping yourself will help your ear tune in to your best pitch and help you mimic and repeat that pitch.

Many female speakers have a tendency to end their sentences in the form of a question when they are nervous or unsure of themselves. We have noticed more and more young women who end even declarative sentences with an upswing in their voice as though they are asking a question. This is abrasive to the listener, especially to an older executive. A question lacks authority and impact. It sounds like this: "Our team will be at the meeting? The customers are happy with our results? Let me know what you think by Tuesday?" Ending each sentence on an upswing can undermine your influence, whether one to one or before a group.

Be Aware of Your Inherited Dialect

Regional dialects and international accents are part of a female's vocal image. Don't get caught not knowing how you sound. If you've recorded yourself or asked a trusted colleague, you are aware of your dialect or accent and you can adapt accordingly. For example, if you are from the East Coast, when presenting elsewhere, prepare to speak a little slower, listen a little more, and include others' opinions a bit more than usual. Have others help you be aware of any curt so-called New Jersey or New York–ness in your tone and mostly in your attitude and carriage. Remember, awareness is 90 percent of the battle. Consider your goal. Do you want your audience to "get" your message, or do you want to risk being dismissed?

If you are a lifelong Southerner, be very careful about your natural dialect if you are speaking outside of your immediate area. Speak a bit more distinctly for northerners present. They really need time to acclimate to your speech pattern. Watch for common Southern idioms like *"y'all"*, *"I declare"*, *"you'n me boy"*, or *"hey!"* (we've heard all of these) that may allow others to dismiss your essential message.

If you have a foreign accent, the audience often assumes you are smarter! Make your words distinct and clear. If you speak Spanish, slow down your English delivery. Remember, all ears need to be primed to your accent. Speak deliberately, and you will be fine—and admired.

Women have some of the most memorable voices on this earth. Consider your favorite politician, performer, or role model. Women's voices are beautiful, individual, passionate, and smart. With continual monitoring and practice, you, too, can have a memorable voice that launches ideas and inspires others. Listen closely to strong female voices you have heard at work. What about them is so distinct? What happens when they speak? How do others respond to them?

To maximize your female voice,

- Record it often. Audio is a speaker's best learning tool. Simple to use, easy to carry, and affordable, recording equipment should be required for every presenter—especially female presenters, who can get caught up in bad habits that undermine their effectiveness.

- Use a microphone to enhance it. Never say no to a mike when you are on site in general, but especially if the acoustics are poor or if you are speaking to a group of more than fifty people.

- Deepen it. Most women benefit from thinking downscale a bit. Practice finding the range of your voice by counting to ten from low to high pitch. Be aware of the middle or comfortable pitch you naturally have. Avoid sounding squeaky by breathing deep. The muscular action in the diaphragm and abdomen creates a column of air that supports the voice and helps create your optimal pitch.

- Use your "standing voice" when you want to have impact. Whether sitting or standing, support your breathing and project your volume so that *all or even one* can hear.

Use your own voice. The women speakers I remember have woven in their own voice. I feel like I know them when they're done or at least they're someone I'd like to know better—they've connected.

Mary Lynn Fayoumi
President and CEO
The Management Association of Illinois

3

Charisma or Credibility? Let Your Audience Choose

The best presenters know how to balance their charisma and credibility. Sometimes this takes time, but it is an essential skill. Too much emphasis on one or the other will affect your intent. The audience will let you know what they prefer. Depending on your profession, you may need to be more or less charismatic up front. Salespeople, for example, tend to respond to a speaker's charisma because they make their living on relationships. However they will also see right through manipulation. Engineers and IT professionals, on the other hand, will be more comfortable with facts, data, and documentation up front; we call this "throwing meat to the audience" first. The effective presenter is able to do this with the right dose of personal style.

Ask about the Audience

How do you learn what the audience wants? Speaking experiences help, but they are not your only educator. You can ask others who have addressed the group what you should expect. You can also call or e-mail selected attendees beforehand. If you're presenting to one person, try to get a feel from the administrative assistant or a coworker about what the person prefers. We once presented to a CEO who required a three-point agenda in advance of all entering his office to speak with him; we found out from his assistant. And if you have established the right trust and rapport, you can ask the audience—even right in the middle—"How does this sound so far?" or "What has been most useful to you at this point?" If you find you've taken an incorrect approach, keep trying to understand their perspective. They will respect that. Follow up with information that more precisely meets their needs.

Women tend to overcompensate in front of male audiences. They never smile, and act as robots, or they turn on the charm a little too much. Avoid these stereotypes. One successful female speaker we know told us that on her speaker evaluation sheets she receives comments like, "You're so real. I love that." She wonders, "Then what in the world is everyone else doing?" Be yourself. Be driven from the inside. Watch female newscasters and note how they use their smiles to engage.

Learn the Language

The language you use creates the impression of real credibility. Tape yourself and be cognizant of the words you use. You'll hear patterns in your speech. Consider these lists:

Weak-Sounding Words to Avoid

Think, wish, hope, problem, wrong, try

I sort of want to maybe

I hope we can

I wish you would

To tell you the truth

I'll be honest with you

More Powerful and Influential Words to Use

Aim, want, will, challenge, right, do

My goal today is to

I am especially excited about

I know that together we can

The reason this is important is . . .

This is key for us today because . . .

When performing the balancing act of credibility and charisma,

- The audience will tell you what they appreciate most. Listen to their verbal and nonverbal responses and adapt accordingly.

- Start with your real self and your best guess based on what you know. Be ready to change paddles midstream and adapt accordingly.

- Practice using the language of influence. It communicates both charisma and credibility.

When I ask consultants to present, I've seen their biographies and credentials. Generally, most people are qualified, but there are people that don't have any spark or any passion or something that makes them special. A lot of training and human resources and organizational development people are doing a lot of the same thing. I'm looking for a flavor other than vanilla.

Diane Kubal
President, Fulcrum Network

4

Be the Storyteller

When you tell stories, you connect head to heart. This is important if you want to be remembered. Your audience buys your ideas based on a feeling they have, and feelings are brought forth from a good story. Stories have a beginning, middle, and end, and they make a point. They can be extended business examples or human-interest stories; use a balance of both, depending on your company's culture. We have observed scientists, engineers, nurses, doctors, executives, creatives, and salespeople respond positively to a speaker's story. The effect is universal, if the story is right. You can also use stories in one on one presentations; they energize the conversation and help you build rapport with your listener.

Stories Are Everywhere

Make note of what happens around you. Try doing it for one day all day long. What comments do clients make? How was your service at lunch? What did the new hire do that was funny? Were your boss's reactions unusual? Did a colleague give you a great idea? If you're alert, you'll find the kernel for great stories and examples in everyday life. Read and let other writers' stories inspire you, though always use your own. A good story is truly yours—unique and absolutely true.

Begin with a Story

A great story or example can anchor the beginning of your presentation. All speakers say, "Thank you for coming." Come up with something more meaningful like this statement that gets right to business: "If you've read a newspaper in the last year, you know how our customers' business has struggled through this economy. Let me share with you what happened to our customer in Toronto last week. . . ." Or ask a question that gets them involved, like this one: "How many of you are finding former customers harder to close this season? The top-ranking woman in our Western Region sales force shared this with me. . . ." If you open with a story or extended example, you will stand out, because almost nobody does.

Tie Story to the Bottom Line

When you list numbers and percentages and qualifications, you tune in to the analytical side, but you lose the emotional side of the idea you're selling. And your audience will recommend, refer, and buy based on feelings . . . about the service, you, or the trust they have around the whole picture. Use your story to get the listener focused on his or her problems or customers, and how you have solved similar problems in the past. Realtors tell us they appreciate it when loan officers who speak to them at luncheons share specific solutions for mortgage issues. You also can tell them how your approach saved a good client, or saved the day! Use specific names and dates only as needed; the key is to communicate the concept. And don't forget to throw in a "what we learned from our mistake" story if it seems appropriate and motivational to the group. Think of the difference between seeing an ad for a new cell phone versus calling three of your best friends who have the new phone. Which will you believe—what the manufacturer paid someone to say or what your colleagues' testimonies reveal?

Use Caution with Personal Stories

Be careful not to tell too many stories about your family. Women can easily fall into this trap and dilute their credibility. Certainly a well-placed clever lesson now and then is acceptable, but an abundance of family stories have their place in other venues—school, church, and parenting or family conferences—to name a few. When you tell any story about your personal experiences outside of work, be certain to tie it to the business point you're making. For example, if you're a marathon runner, explain how what you've learned about endurance is similar to what you've learned with your most demanding customers—endurance pays off at the finish line. Spend more time on the business point than on your marathon feats.

To use stories effectively, learn to

- Fully deliver the emotion of the story. Use the natural heart-tug of the story to make your point. Use your face, voice, and gestures to make it come alive.

- Intersperse your research and documentation with real-life examples that the audience can relate to.

- Look for stories everywhere—both at work and outside it. You never know when the kernel of an experience will help you sell a point or idea.

Take heed and realize that women and others need to hear your stories. So often you marginalize yourself, thinking, "Oh, I'm

just a mom," but it's important to balance life skills with the work
we do; don't minimize either.

> Nanne Finis, RN, MS
> Executive Director, Consulting Services
> Joint Commission Resources

5

Motivate the All-Female Audience

When we ask women for their most challenging experiences when speaking, many will say, "When I have to present to other women." We hear that all-female audiences are difficult, have a different energy, and can be very critical. For a variety of reasons, your all-female audience may be your most difficult one.

Don't ever assume you'll have them in the palm of your hand as you approach the podium. Women tend to be overly critical of other women, especially those presenters who are in a place of power. The podium is a prime example of such a power position. If you're up in front of women, you better have earned it, or else you better be ready to earn respect right in front of them for the first time. If you're presenting one on one to a key female, it's much the same. However, instead of a podium, you've earned the chair across from her desk, and you'll need to prove you're worth her time.

One way to earn respect is to talk about what they want to hear from you. This is a learner-centered approach to tapping into the energy of the room. What you hear will not necessarily change one word of your prepared talk; it will change the way you interact as you speak.

Approach a talk to a key woman or a group of women with humility rather than with ego. Ask questions up front.

What do they find most challenging at work or at home or in their balance of both? What do they want and need to know about their goals? Is this presentation for information, celebration, or for motivation to action?

Of course, those sorts of questions are important for all audiences, but sometimes, women presenting to women forget to take that step because they are overly focused on the details of the presentation itself. Those questions are your pretalk questions gained from your phone interviews. If that is not possible, use the mingling period or meal prior to your talk to speak with a group. Climb into their heads and determine how they are thinking. Listen intently and figure out how they are feeling.

Some very successful female presenters use a story that is easy for others to relate to with some appropriate humor and current cultural references such as movies or television shows. We recommend that you be careful using Oprah and other stars for your quotes. A little here can go a long way. Instead, use someone from the audience that everyone knows—the Chief Executive Officer, Chief Operating Officer, or even the Chief Executive Officer's administrative assistant! Go for stories that are real, down-home, and easy to relate to with every member of the audience. For example, if you work in an industry with a big travel budget but speak to those with less, referring to your recent stay at the Ritz or Four Seasons will probably not be well received. If you travel a great deal and they do not, ditch the airplane story and go for the story of your first impression walking in the door of this conference, how you felt, how you were greeted, who said what to whom.

Whatever you do, always focus on them and on their achievements. Eliminate the word *I* from much of your presentation, even if you are important and have just received an award, and even if they love and respect you. Focus on them to maintain a connection throughout your presentation.

Be Unassuming

Be careful not to sound superior to other women. This is different from being funny and relevant and sharp, because you can relate to some of their female experiences. An air of superiority will come across in a condescending tone or all-assuming stance and will cause defensiveness. If you have an advanced degree that most do not, use examples from your high school or early college days. If you are married and most are not, talk about your dating days. If you have no children and they do, speak of how you love kids or how you admire parenthood. Being unassuming means that you are focusing clearly and closely on the audience because they already told you who they were and what they needed from you. Who you are and what you know is less important.

Sometimes you may be asked to give an award, deliver a eulogy, share a toast, or simply "say a few words" to an all-female group. These are very, very important moments for the audience. They catch a glimpse into who you are quickly and intimately. Be ready for those moments. Have a set of all-purpose stories that are yours and yours alone. What happened to you, how you felt, what you learned, and its application to today's event, will be the best five-minute talk you can give. Especially when you've poured your heart and soul into it.

Know the Female Experience Differs

We once asked a primarily female group of nurses to recall a favorite childhood memory communicating with a relative as part of a warm-up activity. A woman approached us after the session and shared how the activity was difficult for her because she had an unhappy childhood with little communication with any relative. After that, we changed the instructions to, "I'd like for you to think of a time in your past when you communicated memorably with a loved one; go back to your childhood or perhaps an experience you had just last week."

The more experience you have in front of all-female groups, the more you will learn how to walk a fine line between shared experiences and times you may be unknowingly alienating a member of your audience due to background, education, life stresses, children, and so forth. The more open-ended and general you make your questions, allowing for differences in our childhood, our relationships, and our reactions, the better. This is a way to embrace your entire audience.

When you are speaking to a group of women,

> - Prepare for an audience that may be a special challenge to you. Learn about them, and be open to their needs.
>
> - When in doubt, focus on their experiences, all the while relating your experiences to theirs. Always treat your audience as peers.
>
> - Don't get caught in the detail of your slides or notes before you've got a good sense of the big picture outcome for this group of women.

In speaking, one challenge I face is deciding how open to be. I work with a staff that is primarily women. I relate to them in a different way than if it's a predominantly male audience. With women I tell more stories, share more of my personal experience, for example. A male audience responds better when I am more matter of fact. As I've gotten more experienced, I've become more comfortable with taking a risk with an audience on something I feel strongly about—something they may not accept right away or be comfortable with.

> Adrienne Antink, CAE
> VP Component Relations
> Medical Group Management
> Association

6

Look the Part

Most women have had the experience of showing up to an event feeling either under- or overdressed. Usually that's because they didn't have enough information up front; only rarely is it because the information they received was wrong. As a presenter with all eyes upon you, you always need to do your fashion homework. Is fashion savvy noticed? You bet! Ninety-three percent of managers recently polled by OfficeTeam (March 2007) indicated that how employees dress at work influences their chances of earning a promotion.

The choice in how you prepare is up to you. Balance femininity with intelligence. It's no accident, for example, that young female pharmaceutical sales representatives wear conservative suits with sharp shirts and shoulder-length or shorter hair. They're calling on doctors who respect both a healthy female appearance as well as skilled sales ability. While you might get bored dressing all the time within that balance, you can add small touches of your personal style. Express yourself with a great color for your shirts or sweaters or a very pretty shorter-heeled shoe. Carry a bag that is black or brown but represents a designer you love. Spend your money on a great watch or briefcase that spells success. Wear a simple pin that represents your style.

Men Do See Details

Any woman who has ever had a man comment on her jewelry, shoes, perfume, or haircut knows that, contrary to popular belief, men do notice details. For a presenter, details take on added meaning. Nails should be crisp and neat—not long and red. Socks or nylons should always look like new. Shoes should never be scuffed. If the heels are worn down, don't wear them. Jewelry should be very minimal, and earrings should not dangle. Men notice all these things, and your fellow females pay even closer attention.

Save the nail tattoos, the dangling earrings, and the three-inch-high heels for fun time—not for work—and certainly not to present. One image consultant we know suggests that perfume not be worn at work; even a light amount can be distracting to some. Longer hair is fine if it is clipped or tied appropriately. In some creative businesses, like design or fashion, long hair is more accepted. The more conservative your business, the more conservative your hairstyle should be.

Watch Where Their Eyes Dwell

Many women have had to deal with male eyes traveling to an unexpected point on their person. Again, as a presenter you are "on display" at all times. Be cognizant of that. If you see men looking at your legs or chest, make a mental note. What is it you're wearing that's drawing their attention? Do you want or need such attention? Is there a way to minimize the area that seems to be distracting and yet still allow for your femininity to shine through?

Any area you emphasize will be noticed—most often in a distracting way. Do you want to wear your red short-skirted suit? The consequences: Your legs will be noticed, as will how the cut of your figure looks in red. Want to show off your well-toned arms with a sleeveless shirt? You can bet your muscles will be noticed. Do you like the fit of the lower-cut neckline of your new wraparound blouse? You can bet your cleavage will be noticed. Think about what you're emphasizing as you dress. Consider what you can emphasize that stresses your professionalism and your expertise—not your sexuality. When you're finished presenting, do you want the male restroom talk to be, "Wow, she's sexy!" or "Wow, she's a great speaker!" ?

Ask Mentors and Men You Trust

If you have any doubts about whether your choices are correct, ask men who will tell you the truth. Believe it or not, most will do so because they want you to succeed and look a part of their successful team. Don't be shy about asking a male boss what he thinks about your clothing choices. Sometimes men have thoughts but feel too shy to share those thoughts. We know this because when we coach male managers, they ask us for our advice about exactly those issues!

This advice may sound remedial, but in our experience, women are often totally unaware of the impact their clothing or hair is having on their colleagues. Too often, they're following the trends or advice of their friends or partners. When you are confident you have done your best to dress well and appropriately, focus on your message and do a great job of presenting—to both genders.

Fashion reminders for the female presenter:

- Ask both women and men who are not your significant others what they honestly believe about how you dress. Be prepared to hear the truth.

- Make a mental note of any repeated nonverbal or verbal notice of your figure or choices.

- When in doubt, always go for the more conservative choice.

Women don't realize how much work it is to make a good impression. I've heard our managers talking about female presenters from an outside consulting firm who didn't gauge our culture correctly and dressed too risqué.

Lisa Monde
Human Resources Representative
National Association of Realtors

7

Own Your Age

It will happen. You will be the youngest person in the room presenting to your elders. You will not feel particularly comfortable about this situation if you are like most people. However, speaking to an audience that is more mature than you need not be a daunting task if you respect the basic human need to be recognized and understood.

Find the Right Tone

Don't overdo it. Female presenters, especially, get caught in a subservient apology mode, saying, for example, "I am so very, very honored to present to such a distinguished group who have so much more experience than I do in this industry." They already know that. What they do not know, however, is your unique perspective.

We admire our Gen X and Millennial colleagues who impress us with their perspective on media, technology, the Internet, audio and video files, podcasting, blogs, and more. We respect how they set boundaries for balancing a professional life with a personal one. These age groups don't need to feel less experienced when they address us. We assume they have something valuable to add.

It is best to be gracious yet direct with your elders. Veterans and baby boomers like to be appreciated, so it is worth the time to thank them at some point during your presentation if there is a reason that makes sense. For example: "Without the path you struck in 1989, it would be nearly impossible to infiltrate that market today. With that in mind, we make inroads but continue to face challenges."

Before your elders, state what you know to be true. Share it with documentation. Be open to questions and disagreements. Simply tell it like it is for you. Own the opportunity and assume they will benefit from your point of view. Cyndi remembers the "Aha!" she experienced after a day of parenting education led by several thirty-something specialists in teen behavior. These young speakers related not only to parents but also to teens. That perspective could not have been duplicated among her own baby boomer peer network.

Tag! They're It!

We recommend a technique called *tag-and-add* to build trust with anyone, but especially with your senior associates. The technique is simply a repetition of the last few words that the other has said. It is very useful in discussions that follow presentations. Here is an example:

> Senior: "Your theory makes sense in part, but we ran into complications when we tried that with new hires."
> You: "New hires . . . you had some challenges there? Tell me more."

Besides assuring the other that you heard those particular words, it repeats them for the rest of the group. Repeating is helpful for those who may experience hearing loss.

Kick In Your Network

While using the correct tone and tag-and-add are helpful techniques for building a respectful relationship with elders, the absolute most important thing you can do is get to know them. Get to know them all of the time. That way, when you need to speak to them, you can refer to their unique backgrounds and situations. For example: "Carl, you were telling me about the year the building was demolished. Could you remind us what the operations staff learned that year?"

Granted, some older workers tend to talk too much. Seniors receive a bad reputation for that in many organizations. Still, engaging the older personnel in your company is important; set a time frame for talking. Always find a few more minutes to ask them about their personal life or anything non-work-related. Many have grandchildren who delight them. It is smart to tap into the whole person at work, no matter their age!

When your audience is older than you,

- Don't push it by overcomplimenting them. Don't apologize for being younger or less experienced.

- Don't assume you know what they'll say or do. Reach out to them beforehand. Get to know them every day.

- Honor their comments. Recognize their accomplishments. Let others hear, too.

When I think of challenges earlier on, it was gaining credibility and rapport, especially when I was in a room of thirty-something aggressive sales guys. I was in my twenties, and it was easy for them to take the floor from me. Since then, I've learned rapport-building techniques like storytelling—especially using examples of things I've run across in other programs I've presented and who I am personally. Inexperienced women overprepare and focus too much on the content—the management practices and human resource policies—and they fill every moment; they never want to veer off course. It's as if they want a squeaky-clean agenda rather than going where the audience wants to go. I think it's because they don't want to show vulnerability.

> Mary Lynn Fayoumi
> President and CEO
> The Management Association of Illinois

8

Be Memorable

Things will go wrong around you. In fact, the most common challenge for a speaker once she is in front is not the audience; it's the environment. Starting late, not being heard because of poor acoustics, managing a hot or cold room or too large or small a crowd—all these challenges happen all the time. You can still be memorable and even more effective if you follow some simple reminders.

We watched a female presenter give a fifteen-minute talk where absolutely everything possible went wrong . . . except for her! She remained memorable despite the forces of the universe conspiring against her. Her laptop quit midway, her boss then spent the rest of her talk trying to fix it in front of the room, two colleagues began a conversation midway through her program, and she forgot her second major point. But, ultimately, she won. She gave one of the best speeches of the day. She remained focused, unflustered (on the outside), and in control of the room.

Stay on Track

She was a memorable presenter because she stayed firmly on message with a calm expression, lively eyes, a warm smile, no apologies, and when the technology failed, she moved effortlessly to her flipchart. She firmly and encouragingly let her boss know she didn't need his help (especially in the front of the room!). When she forgot her second point, she simply asked the audience what they felt was "missing" from part one in order to effortlessly fill in the blanks.

The audience remembered that presentation because it was so well handled. Despite the problems she encountered, she handled her audience well, focused her message, and appeared unflappable.

Use Your Wit and Your Audience

Speakers are continually faced with challenges that often are out of their control—for that moment. It's how you handle the difficulties that the audience remembers. When the loud alarm blares in the middle of the presentation you've worked on for weeks, use your humor: "Darn it! I knew they'd catch me someday," or "Is that recess?" When the lights go out, say, "I was going for a relaxed atmosphere. . . ." When the computer dies, try something like this: "This was a test—only a test. And now we'll return to our normal programming—paper handouts!"(You have hard copy available just in case.) Use your own style and humor to deal with those situations. The idea is to move forward. Most of the audience wants to move on. They don't want you to waste their time by apologizing. In fact, savvy audience members will often help you. We've had people behind video cameras, at our laptops, at the podium console, searching for outlets, and discovering heating and cooling apparatus for us . . . all at a moment's notice!

When the room is crowded, don't make a big deal of it. Just give more frequent breaks or allow the group to participate and ask questions more often. When there is almost nobody present, move forward as if you had a full house. We firmly believe the right person is in the room. The several who are present want to feel honored and important—not "less than."

When you're starting late, move forward and cut about 20 percent of your content. There is no way you will be able to do the presentation you planned in less time; too often we've seen speakers rush through everything. Women do this even more than men—most likely because they feel responsible for all the details. Instead, put on your editor hat quickly, and talk less.

To always be a memorable presenter,

- Stay calm, even if things don't go exactly as planned.

- Don't apologize. Move it forward, instead.

- Connect with your audience, and trust that your connection with them will help get you through the worst.

Women still feel we have that much more to prove. We always try to be perfect in every way. It's hard to keep it all together like that all the time. I've learned that it's okay to be confident, but you don't have to be all-knowing all the time.

Lisa Monde
Human Resources Representative
National Association of Realtors

PART 2

Adapt with Professionalism

9

Maneuver the Dotted-Line Relationship

While all relationships require that we cooperate with the other person, some of our relationships have an innate power structure built into them. For example, you take what your boss says seriously because she is your superior in the relationship. This is the person who will evaluate you, reward you, and promote you. She has the ultimate authority. You will also listen closely to someone you consider to be a topic expert. This person, like a favorite professor, has an authority that springs from his or her knowledge and the usefulness of that knowledge to you and your work. You may also defer to an executive at your company who has more insight on a particular issue. When he or she speaks, you listen because the executive has a special set of eyes and ears to the issue at hand and high value in solving the issue. We tend to rank people mentally based on who has the most authority, whom we must defer to, and from whom we take orders.

If we don't like a person "above" us at work—if they don't treat us with respect, if they are not credible in our eyes—we "appear" to give them authority, but in reality we are probably not impressed with them, and as such we will not follow their directives, understand their vision, and perhaps we will even resist their leadership.

Regardless of whether it is our boss, a topic expert, or a senior executive, we decide how we choose to give authority to our leaders. This inner yes or no will significantly impact our response to the leader and therefore our relationship with them. When it is our boss, we call this a solid-line relationship, since we report directly to this person. On the flowchart, there is no doubt who reports to whom.

There is another kind of work relationship, that of the dotted line. In this situation we have a direct working relationship, but not a reporting relationship. We influence and affect one another, we attend meetings together, we plan and partner, but we are not in a traditional way accountable to one another.

In some ways, this is also known as the informal network. While we have an official flowchart at work, there is also a chart within the chart. This chart within the chart may reveal not only the solid and dotted lines, but also the "real" communication that goes on within the organization. Perhaps one person used to work for another and no longer does, but holds great weight with them in terms of expert authority. Still another may be the repository of all that is new with both the rumor mill as well as with breaking news. Regardless of the relative rank, privilege, position, or salary, that informal network is often much more relevant and influential than is the formal network.

It is important, of course, to understand the formal network. Who is your boss, and what does he or she want? How will they measure your performance? How can you help them achieve their goals with their own boss? Understand that the informal network is vital as well. Build your bridges between formal and informal networks daily. You will be crossing them frequently in the future.

While navigating your solid-line relationships will be challenging at times, it is the dotted-line relationships that often pose the greatest difficulty because there is no direct authority. If I am in a dotted-line relationship to you, I don't "have" to do what you want. As psychiatrist Rudolf Dreikurs taught, "Cooperation can never be required, it can only be won." Your job in any dotted-line relationship is to win cooperation—for yourself and for your boss.

Dotted-line relationships are all a bit different. For example, you may have no clear line of real authority, yet you are in a clear relationship with the other person, each having to influence the other in some way. And whether it is a relationship with a peer, another department leader, a vendor, a consultant, or even a customer, remember that you are mutually influencing one another.

Your personal involvement in these relationships is the key to their success. You can be a technical wizard, scientifically and professionally correct, but if you don't win in the relationship, you will not have won the cooperation. And when you win with the relationship, you draw a faint line through the dots and link them in an ever-closer way! That is connectivity at work. Questions and quick phone calls, heads-ups and FYIs, as well as interest in the family and personal pursuits are all ways to keep your ties to those who are not connected directly to you by means of the formal network and flowchart.

The famous defense attorney Clarence Darrow remarked that the job of the defense attorney is to make his client likable to the jury. When we like someone personally, when they take an interest in us, and when they know the names of our children and our pets, it is very difficult to be obstructive with them, even when we disagree. Your work with your "dotted lines" is to establish all your relationships so that you are liked for your interest in others, respected for your knowledge and authority, and relied upon for your delivery of what you promise. Navigate and maneuver in those ways, and you will build strong bridges for many years.

Speaking Up

Speaking up is especially important when you are giving a presentation or an update in front of one of your dotted-line relationships. Be aware that it may be a moment of influence few can resist. You want to make sure that the person you are attempting to influence clearly hears that you understand their side, that you know their read on the situation, and that their essential message is within your words. That is the power of going to the other, not requiring them to come to you. For women, bridging gaps is more of a natural tendency than it is for men—one must attempt to nurture and understand the workings of another person. It may be your hidden skill or an apparent one. Know that understanding is a key force for all persuasion. It is the first moment of the mutual yes.

You'll need to draw upon extraordinary understanding, patience, and wit. Through the personality—perhaps *only* through the personality—the message is driven home. When you want to influence another, don't be afraid to dive deep into understanding them personally. By this we mean your understanding of what is "really" important to them, even what is "really" important to them at this particular meeting. Especially in conflict, be aware of those values. And resist being self-defensive. To take things "personally" at work is a waste of time and effort, and it puts you in a vulnerable position. No matter how much it may hurt your pride or feelings, always go toward the other, and gain understanding when in conflict. The president of High Point University, Nido Qubein, cautions that hostility is always related to fear. Barking dogs do not want to fight; they are merely afraid. When we pass them by, they secretly say to themselves in dog language, "It sure is good I barked. They left without incident!" That is not unlike the behavior of our colleagues! Being good at what you are good at is only the beginning. Be good at being interested in what *they* are good at, and in doing so promote your potential to influence. When we understand, we can influence better.

Use your female powers of connection to relate in a personal way. Your bonding overtures are more important than the logic of your argument. In the end, people like doing business with people they like doing business with. Wars have been averted on a handshake, agreements reached through likability, and some of your colleagues simply like the way you are with them. When that happens, you have won the greatest of victories—trust.

To best connect with others,

- Honor those with whom you are in a dotted-line relationship. Keep them aware and in the loop. Ask and question them. Never surprise them. Be a true and trusted colleague, one they can count on.

- Be keenly aware of the fact that through your presentations you have access to them in an entirely different way. They have an opportunity to see your effect on others they respect. That perspective may be just enough to make the transition to cooperation. Your presentations, even your short ones, are critical to building trust. Like it or not, if you are a good presenter, you are likely to be more easily believed.

- Never fail to credit them and your "partnership" with them. Make sure that at every turn you act as if they are already in alignment with you in your "partner" references. Don't speak for them, but make sure you include them early and often. Be genuine, never phony. Always appreciate what others do, even when it is what they are supposed to do. That is what bridges are made of.

Don't go in thinking, "I am going to wow them with absolutely all the statistics of this situation." Instead, be relaxed and be who you are. I think sometimes women tend to want to impress with the facts and avoid the personalization because they don't want to be perceived as too soft. But sharing a compelling story— opening up your own life a little bit—helps connect.

> Judy Schueler
> Vice President-Chief Learning Officer
> Abrazo Healthcare

10

Survive When the Audience Is Just Not That Into You

There will be times when you love your presentation more than the audience did, or those awful times when they know and you know that you really bombed. How can you save yourself when you know you are not as prepared as you should be, not as confident as you want to be, and not as successful as you hoped to be?

Actually we never really know if we received a failing grade until it is all over. Some in your audiences will like you so much that even during a lackluster performance, they will be rooting for you. Others will be so engaged in your material that they will overlook your flawed presentation. Others, however, are influenced by how you do what you do, how you say what you are saying, and how your preparation is reflected in your delivery. Bosses, mentors, competitors, rivals, and customers are among this group.

It is important to begin inside yourself. Any problem you encounter is best seen as feedback, rather than failure. Each time you present, you can learn to present even better next time. With that attitude, you can avoid much of the pain of negative feedback by converting it into redemption the next time. We all fail. Not all of us, however, get up the next day determined to do better. Perseverance is the measure of those who succeed.

Therefore, seek engagement with the audience and their needs early on. Watch the other speakers who are going before you. See what is working with this group and what is not connecting with them. Getting to the meeting early is a good strategy only if you use the time well. Some presenters don't attend the prior presentations due to nerves or lack of interest. That is an error of classic proportions. When you know what the audience knows (the presentation prior to yours) and you have seen what the audience has not seen (themselves responding to that presentation), then you have more ways to engage them early and often.

Professionals will often tell a story they know the audience will respond to with humor or engagement. That's called a signature story—a story the speaker uses time and time again. One CEO of a hospital founded by three German Roman Catholic nuns in the early 1800s continually spoke of their journey, their courage, their determination. Whenever he wanted his staff to emulate a characteristic, he would speak of the "nuns." Each time, he revealed a bit more of their history, their personality. Only he truly "owned" this story.

If you attend the presentation prior to yours, you can tag on to the other presenter and then add your part to it. This tag-and-add technique is very helpful in showing the audience the relationship of the two presentations and allows for the audience to connect quickly with you.

Sometimes presenters attempt to tag-and-add with their opening remarks. "Thank you, Jane, for that great presentation. Wasn't she great, everyone? Let's give her another round of applause! Now, in my presentation . . ." This is a *mistake* and a very amateurish way to use vital information. The audience already applauded; they don't need to do so again. They are ready to hear you. Don't make them wait.

And don't make them compare you to the prior presenter, even if in a flattering way.

Instead begin with "meat," something they can chew on early in your presentation that signals to the audience, "This person is worth listening to!" Then, later, when you get to a main point, you can insert, almost as an aside, "One of the things I loved about Jane's presentation was her emphasis on seeing things through the customer's eyes first and foremost. I want us all to keep Jane's perspective clearly before us. . . ." What a much more sophisticated approach, clearly one that's more effective for the audience and for your message. It honors Jane for her wisdom but does not take the spotlight off you. Use that technique even if Jane hit a giant home run and you feel your presentation pales in comparison. Do so with confidence.

Develop some signature stories from your own experience. They need not be perfect, only apropos to the situation and always from your own viewpoint. Just be careful not to fall in love with your story so much that you push it into presentations where it does not belong. Be careful of stories about your children, your cat or dog, or your graduate work or alma mater. You can use them—just don't *overuse* them. It is better to speak to what the audience has in common, not what is only about you.

Be ready also to tag-and-add when you can. Just be careful not to do so in a syrupy sweet way that looks ingratiating. Make what they said or did part of your material, not your material part of them. Stay with your own authority. Kevin once presented to three thousand operating-room nurses directly after General Colin Powell. In that speech to nurses, General Powell told a heartwarming story of how an operating-room nurse saved his son's life. All Kevin thought he could do was quickly try to figure out how a nurse saved two of his son's lives! Instead he relied on a mentor who had told him many years ago, "Be you."

If you fear disengagement, consider audience participation—a very useful technique, especially when the audience members have a great deal in common as far as their interests and expertise. Break the audience up into groups of two or three to weigh in on the topic. Do this by saying, "Stand up and find one or two people who are not currently sitting next to you." This tactic will provide stimulation and puts everyone on high alert. Give them a focus question, and tell them how much time they will have. You will achieve three things: time to breathe and regroup, refreshing the audience, and even more relevant material to move ahead with. Participation, talking, and movement always engage an audience more than you standing up there trying desperately to say something meaningful! When they finish in their groups, simply ask for someone to summarize or share one thing that they had in common. You take notes on the flipchart and then tag-and-add to the comments. Audiences really like participating. It can be unnerving the first times you do it, but it always works. Just make sure that they get up and find new people to talk to, never pair them with the persons next to them.

The same approach goes when halfway through your presentation you are seeing eyes close, animosity appear, and group conversations happen. Put them into groups. Go to your very best friend—the flipchart—and brainstorm some ideas. Find out what your audience members are thinking and what you most need to address in your presentation. Don't fear questions: simply ask the question back to the audience and chart their answers and contributions. Don't fear their animosity; get it out in the open. Don't become annoyed with their side conversations; just get them into new groups! By doing so, you will be perceived as the master of the moment and as someone who is open to these ideas and not de- fensive. Resist coming across as defensive—it never looks good on you. Always be inquisitive instead. Be open in front of them. You can always cry later!

End early when things are going well. Audiences like it when they are really in the zone with you and you leave them wanting more. This is referred to as the Zeigarnik ef- fect and states that people remember uncompleted or inter- rupted tasks better than completed ones. Ending early only increases their desire for more of you! Especially if your au- dience has been drinking too heavily, end early. You are fighting something beyond your control, and they won't remember you anyway!

Whether the audience is into you or not, never, ever, never go beyond your allowed time. It is the rank amateur or the arrogant professional who will say, "May I take a few extra minutes? . . ." If there is a mortal sin in speaking, this is it! The audience will never tell you they hate it, but they do, and as soon as you say it, they will begin to zone out. End exactly on time to the minute or end early. Those are the only two al- ternatives for the influential professional—you!

Keep learning more about your audience. Talk to them, in- terview them, attend the lunch or dinner prior to your talk with them, and use names in your presentation of those in the audience. All these techniques will help you avoid a cri- sis. Like your dotted-line relationships, the more of a rela- tionship you have with an audience, the more they like you and the more they will root for you and help you succeed.

When you speak often enough, you will eventually wind up in venues that are awful for presentations and don't allow you to shine. Pillars, loud music from the wed- ding next door, bright sunlight, poor lighting, squeaky chairs, waiters running here and there, audiovisual techni- cians who want to change your microphone battery as you speak, long rectangular rooms, and more will become both your nightmare and your reality at some point. When those things happen, change what you can and adapt to what you cannot. In every case, move as close to the audience as possible. Step off the stage, walk the aisles, and remain near your audience. Do whatever you can to keep the audience interested. Always, always avoid complaining or looking annoyed. Remain devoted to your audience. Be extremely respectful and gracious with your audiovisual staff—they can make or break your performance. Watch your sarcasm or pessimism, be very stingy about referring to the noises. The more you do, the more apparent those distractions become.

When your audience is just not that into you,

- The layout of the room, poor lighting, or noise next door may be the real problem. When you know the audience well, you may also know that there are some firings going on, the company's stock numbers are down, or there has been a death on the team. A poor reception is not always about you. Adapt as best you can.

- Always know that you have options and that you can proceed with your presentation in a way you haven't necessarily planned. On the way to the presentation, review the main points you want the audience to understand clearly. Preparation will allow you to make sure these points are delivered despite any issues that may crop up.

- End on time or end early—never end later, never!

Being real is important. It allows you to establish a relationship. Great women speakers catch our attention, are very dynamic, have a presence, and are very confident.

I find that women can sabotage themselves by being too

quick to admit that they think they are not quite the expert the audience might believe them to be . . . giving away confidence before they start.

Women can also agree too much, giving up the stage, with the audience wondering, Is everything the "right" answer?

Jill Berry Bowen, RN, CHE
VP Patient Care Services
Mercy Health System

11

Handle Criticism

"Women take things too personally." We've heard that claim many times from both female and male leaders in our coaching and consulting work. Perhaps you've also been told not to "take it personally." Interestingly, men don't seem to have to be reminded to be objective as much as women do. Men certainly take things personally, but they have also been taught to turn those feelings outward with action, anger, or annoyance. Women have been taught that a negative outcome is perhaps their fault, their failing, or a result of their faulty thinking, and thus they turn inward for solace or solution. The first thing to remember when you are confronted with difficult situations when presenting or facilitating is to consider the source of the negativity. Most likely poor reaction is due to changes in rules or in the alignment of expectations, or to some feeling related to either. Unaligned goals often manifest themselves in resistance. Consider being joined to another by a rope. If the other is going one way and you the other, the ultimate "tug" you feel is called resistance. That resistance creates a conflict, and a tug-of-war develops. Not unlike corporate communications, that power struggle, while obvious if we see the rope, is quite invisible when the rope is not perceived. Invisible, yes, and also quite apparent. When you are confronted, resist pulling. Instead, draw closer.

Many times those who complain about us or to us are simply frustrated that they cannot solve the dilemma by themselves, and so they train their sights on us. When they complain, what you do "next" is important. Resist the temptation to submit or to run. Go closer. Handle things in the here and now—ask a question, paraphrase, empathize, and explain your point of view. Resist the temptation to fight, flee, or freeze—all normal instincts. These normal instincts are not useful when you want to lead, influence, and present. You need to accomplish a fourth *F*—"figure it out." Despite what reality TV shows want us to believe, real leaders and influencers rarely win by brute force. They win through a mutual yes over time, accomplished with caring dialogue.

Use Honest Awareness

When Cyndi was a fledgling communications trainer, she presented one of her first workshops to a small local insurance company. The reception was colder than she'd expected, and she worried that she hadn't met her clients' needs. Her superior suggested she take the client to lunch, and so she did. That was also the first time she took a client to lunch! She walked into the restaurant with trepidation, ready to receive an onslaught of criticism. Instead, her client thanked her in a friendly manner, and within the first ten minutes said, "Yeah, I'm glad you were there that day. We had a major staff member quit, and everybody was depressed." Cyndi never forgot that great illustration of what can happen when you focus too much on yourself and not enough on asking questions and clarifying the specific issues of others. Without being willing to go to lunch, she never would have "really" known what was going on.

In retrospect, were she back in front of that group, she would have gained awareness of their problem by checking in with them: "I have asked a few questions, and it appears as if there are not a lot of answers. When this happens, I usually like to stop and ask if there is something you'd like me to know. How does what we're talking about fit in with your life at work today?" Check-in statements that let the group know that you know that things are different or difficult can build trust and an honest exchange of information. Select the question based on the type of group. If the group is primarily male, be less feeling-focused and more oriented toward strategy and thinking; for example, you might say, "Please tell me how this strategy is working for you," "I'm interested in hearing your thoughts on this strategy." This technique also works well for female audiences who are in the technical or medical fields. The solicitation is warm, and the desired results focus on the strengths of the audience, which is thinking. It is certainly fine to ask feeling questions of scientific and engineering types after they give you their thoughts—the mode in which they feel more certain.

You can also ask the feeling question in a disguised, more easily digestible form. For example, you begin with "What are your thoughts about our strategy for rolling out Alpha-629?" After you record the answers, then ask the feeling question: "How do you feel that is working for us?" Or you can disguise it even more: "What do you think our customers will feel about it?" Or more plainly: "How do you feel about it?"

Feeling questions help move things along because feelings are the fuel that moves us. While our logic may forecast the vision and the details, our feelings provide the impetus. For example, impulse items we buy at the grocery store are rarely tied to our logic. In fact, they are often right at the cash register so we'll buy them with no logic whatsoever! Chocolate, Hollywood gossip, weight-loss booklets, and holiday pins are all ready and waiting for us—at the checkout. Uncover the feelings with skill, and you'll begin to better align goals.

Listen When You Ask or Don't Ask

It is frustrating to be in the audience, hear a speaker ask an open-ended question (one that cannot be answered with a simple yes or no) of the audience, but then proceed without allowing the audience to offer their answers. Some presenters answer the question themselves! For example, we once heard a presenter ask, "Can anyone in the audience relate to having a teenage daughter? Well, I know I sure can. We have three, and let me tell you, they're a handful." Imagine the difference in connectedness if she had waited to hear the unique experiences of her audience. She could have played off the content, the humor, and the rapport.

Sometimes, an audience member will be negative or will be extremely quiet about an issue under discussion. A skilled facilitator always recognizes this and attempts to rectify the problem. Where is the pain? What is the fear? This is a tricky area because, while you want to probe, on the one hand, you also want to stay in control. If you use less intimidating phrasing such as, "It sounds as if . . . ," "It appears to be . . . ," and "Let's take the pulse of the group to check . . . ," you will be successful at staying in control and yet gentle enough to encourage.

During a period of questioning and listening, the female presenter needs to be aware of body language. You do not need to smile during a difficult exchange, but you must look alert and confident. Avoid crossing your legs, arms, and feet, or playing with your hair or jewelry. When you are listening, stay still. When you respond, move a bit closer to the audience member speaking. This body language creates a sense of intimacy and response without crowding or getting "too close." Both standing still and moving closer convey confidence.

The female presenter's goal is to be seen as firm and friendly. Firmness shows respect for you, and friendly shows respect for them. Respect is the real issue in conflict, and it is likely at the root of many issues that come up in your presentations. You will be cut off, not listened to, talked over, interrupted, your point will be wildly misinterpreted, or you will even be personally attacked. While no presenter wants any of those things to happen, you must be prepared so that you succeed by memorably handling the situation and the person.

When under fire, remember to

- Ask questions to get at the real threat. Presenters often tend to operate on assumptions and jump to conclusions. Only the audience knows for sure how they are feeling. Take the time to find out how they feel without undue delays in the program. If it is important to them, it needs to be important to you also.

- Listen when you hear an answer. Really listen. You may have to change your agenda to accommodate the audiences' needs. Beware of being distracted. If listening is an issue for you, go to the flip chart and use the exact words the person is using, not all of them, but enough of them to show that you listened. Now you have a record of the words, the audience member is satisfied they were heard, and you can use the flip chart as notes to yourself.

- Be a keen observer of how others act when they are defensive, and rather than be critical of them, attempt to see "what else" they could have done. Remember it is the "next" thing that you do that is critical to your response being perceived as defensive or useful to the audience.

A good presentation is one that is well structured, sequenced, and not overrehearsed. I prefer not to go through "formal" preparations when presenting. The typical process that I use is to start with a meaningful story or an anecdote, focus on key take-aways, and end with a strong close.

> Michelle Gadsden-Williams
> Vice President and Global Head
> Office of Diversity & Inclusion
> Novartis Pharma AG

12

Keep Your Tiger in Check

You don't want to be seen as the shrew who needs to be tamed while the group watches your angry outbursts. When you encounter something that angers you, remember what Kevin tells his coaching clients, "Someone else doesn't make you angry; you make you angry." When anger erupts, control, control, control. This does not mean you need to deny anger; it means you must remember it is you who makes you mad and it is you who makes you cope. It is your choice. Choose then to purposely delay your instinctive, less useful response by waiting a few seconds, literally three or four seconds. This will allow a breath, and it allows the audience to breathe as well. Another choice is to paraphrase without sarcasm or judgment. Simply paraphrase, even repeat, what the person has said. Often they will agree and further clarify, sometimes apologize for their harshness. You take notes on the flip chart. Then do something unexpected—agree with them! The famous psychiatrist, Alfred Adler said, "I always agree with my patients." At the time he was treating some pretty crazy people, yet he knew that if he didn't go to where they were, they would never be so inclined to come to where he was.

Simply begin with, "I agree this is a tricky topic (this is a difficult issue) (that we have to put the customer first, etc.)." Then never use the word *but* after you begin, rather use the word *and*. Therefore, you might say, "I agree with you, Bob, that this is a critical time and that we have strong feelings about the strategy, and I would like to give you another option to consider. . . ." The use of the word *but* is disconnective and always engenders a fight even if only an interior one. The word *and* joins and connects as well as allows room for the consideration of a new idea without voiding the previous idea. Watch smooth presenters: they rarely fight—they disagree with style.

Sometimes those incidents that seem unrelated to our business life are often central to it. Cyndi remembers being on a completely full flight to Orlando, Florida, to a large convention. Everyone else in the universe seemed to be heading there as well. Feeling lucky she had an aisle seat from which to stretch throughout the flight, she warily eyed the one empty middle seat next to her as the plane boarded, wondering if it would fill. Surely, just as the flight attendants were making their last announcements, a harried young man stood above her, eyed the remaining middle seat, and said, "Oh, boy! The middle seat! I was hoping for this!" with a big smile. It was hilarious at the time and struck her as such a great attitudinal adjustment to what for most people is a huge annoyance. Of course, that opened up a conversation that lasted all the way to Orlando. He could have complained or been irritated. But what if Cyndi was his new customer or she was the new boss he was about to meet, or what if he was the one to interview her? Remember, we like to do business with people we like to do business with. While complainers may be right, they are often looked upon with distrust and disconnection. Few of us want to be around them. Save your complaints for home—they will love you anyway!

Sometimes your audience will complain. Sometimes they will look like they are going to complain. That's normal. Audiences are like us: They get annoyed, angry, and aggravated. Resist the temptation to let them influence how you feel. Let them instead inform you of the need to adapt. You may find this a good time to keep moving, or it might be time for a "break" for ten minutes, and still at other times you may want to put audience members in small groups for a focused discussion on a topic or question of your choosing. The point is not to allow the angry person or the angry outburst to hijack your meeting or your agenda. While we find these digressions to be very unusual, they do happen.

One great coping technique is the "parking lot," which is written on a flipchart. Collect questions that are out of bounds or statements that are likely to take you away from your goal. Simply say, "Thank you for that. Is it okay with you if we put that in the parking lot and if we get a moment later or during the break, we can revisit it?" Don't wait for a reply; just go right to the flipchart, write their concern verbatim, rip the sheet off, and put it on the wall away from direct sight—in a corner, on the sidewall, or the like. Then promptly forget it. *Parking lot* really means, "vast graveyard of ideas we will never revisit again!" But only you know that!

Adjust Your Attitude on the Spot

Adjust your attitude when you feel anger rising up and you're the one speaking or facilitating the group. Acknowledge that you feel angry to yourself; this will allow you to deal with the strong emotion better. Don't deny it; just know it. Don't let loose just at the moment. Save it for later—for a heart-to-heart talk with a dear friend or colleague or your boss.

The key principle here is that the audience really doesn't care what you think—they care what they think, and if you listen to it without judgment, the negative issue or outburst will pass or be responded to by others. Resist the temptation to say too much—if anything—about what you feel. They probably don't care, and your stand will cause more problems for you down the road. As the presenter, you have a special role. They came to hear you, and they want to hear themselves. They want to agree, to nod with you, to know—and they are eager to respond in some way.

Keep your cool, and maintain nondefensive body posture. Repeat a mental mantra such as, "This too shall pass" or "This is not the worst thing." At the workplace, amicable relationships must continue, because you will see your "foe" again and again. If you honor differences, hold your outbursts, and breathe deeply, it will be easier to face the contentious person tomorrow.

When anger wells up, remember that

- Nonverbal communication "tells on you." Keep your face and body calm. Bring out the adult in you—not the two-year-old. The audience wants you in control. They do not want to see the inner you at this moment, no matter how "right" you are.

- Tomorrow will be another day, and the difficult person will still be around. Thank the person for his or her opinion, acknowledge good points that were made, and move forward. Then have lunch with your difficult person to further your dotted-line relationship. Remember the lunch Cyndi had? There may be a lunch like that waiting for you also.

- Don't fall into the female trap of overemotionalizing, especially when all eyes are on you! You may feel the drama, you may feel unfairly criticized, you may even be "right"—the audience doesn't care, they just want you to be useful to them in the moment. That is called high value.

With anger, it is fine to let the audience know that you are appropriately angry, and that you have every right to be. You need to let hecklers know that they are off-base right away and not welcomed. . . . Cut them off and let them know this is not appropriate behavior. I have used humor to win them over and that works in about 30 percent of the cases. Hecklers usually just want to be the smartest guys in the room; make it clear to them that they are not.

Tim McNamara, PharmD
Vice President, Clinical Research and
　　Medical Affairs
ISTA Pharmaceuticals
Irvine, CA

13

Be Professional—Even When Your Boss Is Not

You may be asked to present with your boss, especially early in your career. The most common problem we hear when women talk to us about copresenting with a boss— either male or female—is that it is difficult to get a word in. Some considerations when you are copresenting with your boss include the type of relationship you have with your boss, why she or he wants you to copresent, and what the expectations are.

Since the boss has the power position, the audience naturally lends their ears his or her way. But you also have power—a listening power that can go beyond what the boss is able to perceive from the audience. Presenters often neglect to "listen" to the audience, and therefore they miss cues the audience is giving them nonverbally, in the form of questions, even in the form of the audience's inattention. In the world of work today, listeners win. As your boss presents, watch the audience and notice what is being said and unsaid by your boss. Be ready to add on to the topic. Always be ready even if you are not called upon. Regardless of your status or power base, the key skill of listening is the one skill you will use every day to survive and thrive. Listen to the content and the intent of your boss, mention it, and then add on to it.

Listen and Understand What Is Not Said

When you are in a situation where you are copresenting and feeling left out, just listen. When your boss pauses after a point, indicate what you see and hear. For example, you might say something like, "I notice many of you nodding when Ms. Sampson indicated that the budget forecast looked challenging. What budget constraints are you feeling that we may not be aware of?" Clear this one ahead of time with your boss so that he or she will truly be open to what is coming from the audience. If this gets no audience response or if they are quiet by nature, put them in small groups and seek feedback that way. This allows for discussion and for a somewhat anonymous feedback—perceived safety for the individual.

Or, "I join Ms. Sampson in her assessment of the situation; I'm wondering if we could see a show of hands that indicates your agreement." Remember, this is risky if you are not sure you'll get a good show of hands. Don't chance this unless you are sure you'll get support.

Or, "Ms. Sampson, while you've presented this, many have been smiling and nodding. Why do you think this is this getting such a favorable response?" Avoid making this look rehearsed, or it will not be seen with much authority.

These scenarios illustrate how to facilitate the presentation with the audience. Beware of looking like a "goody-goody" as you do this. Yes, you want to support your boss. You also want to maintain your own integrity. One way to do that is to stand elsewhere in the room—off to the side, in back, away from the primary presenter—and as you ask the questions, be closer to the audience physically than the presenter is. This makes you appear to be one of them, much like an interviewer would be.

Consult with One More Idea

You can even practice a copresentation so that it is clearly planned that one of you will always have one more idea. The "one more idea" technique keeps you memorable. It shows added thought, savvy, and caring. This is called value, and people remember those who are valuable to them. Your boss will likely not have a great deal of time or the inclination to rehearse fully, so make sure that you bullet-point your ideas for clearance to clearly and quickly give your boss access to your intended content.

For example, if in the presentation you have outlined six ways to combat client objections to your product, you can conclude on the spot with one more idea based on audience reactions and feedback. "Many of you have indicated that you would like more flexibility in pricing. Another way this can work with the client, as Mary has pointed out, is to follow up with an e-mail summary that adds one more new price work-up. Let's take a moment and discuss the advantages and disadvantages of this approach for your business." The one-more-idea technique is most effective when used unexpectedly; it becomes a bonus that is unique to you.

Additionally you can be the summarizer for the meeting, making sure that the opinions and ideas are noticed, recorded, and considered. This advocacy gives the audience the feeling that the boss is listening through you.

Engage with Respect, Awareness, and Caution

When copresenting with a boss, whether in front of a group or over a business lunch, it is always important to proceed with confident caution. You want to assert your presence and talents but, more important, showcase the unique talents of your boss. The boss always wants to look good, and not only for his or her own purposes. When the boss looks good, it is good for the entire team when viewed by the boss's boss. That success protects your team's budget, enhances the usefulness of the team to the corporation, and puts the results of the team squarely in the forefront.

You are prepared to take on the role of engager. Do so by subtly mentioning your own work, while also acknowledging the leadership of your boss. For example: "Sam, I noticed you are working with elderly employees in the customer service call center. Ms. Delveccio and I have had some great positive inroads here, and our challenge is finding those who want to work full-time. What thoughts do you have on this issue of full-timers?"

Or, "Fred, the first thing I remember Ms. Riccardo saying to me about our account with you is that you are growing well in new technology. How is it that you do this?" (In essence, you can shine when the boss may not or doesn't want to—if you blend cautious assertiveness with constant listening.)

One final note: Find out how your boss wants to be referred to, both in general and at this meeting. Depending on the audience, you may need to use the title *Doctor*, when in the office you'd call her Kate. One senior physician executive recently asked his entire team of nonphysicians to stop calling him Dr. He said it made him feel somewhat special, and he wanted to feel more like "a team member." His team actually fought him on it until he implored them. Adapt here, and do so taking into account a discussion with your boss.

When you are copresenting with your boss,

> • Prepare and memorize some good "lines" you can use as needed. These lines should be content-related. Remember, if conflict develops, use none of these to "get even." Use them only to engage and elicit cooperation. Always honor

attendees—you will see all of them again, and they will re-member how they were treated even when they've forgotten what you said long ago.

- Never allow anyone else to determine how you will respond. You will have more influence if you are the decision maker for how you will act. Control is especially critical when you present and aim to influence.

- Respect your boss's authority while also allowing yourself to shine. Debrief with your boss afterwards, and return feed-back, beginning, of course, with what they did well.

In the advertising field, you make a lot of team presentations. Different departments work together: There's typically a cre-ative person, a digital expert, a media strategist, and a re-search person. When you're pitching a new client, you have to go through all the components of the communications mix. As a team, you have to look like you work together . . . and enjoy it.

Mary Krueger
Director of Strategy
Prometheus

14

Survive—Even on a Bad-Hair Day

At least once in your career, you will be scheduled to give an important presentation on one of the worst "bad-hair" days of your life. The traffic is horrendous, your assistant is out sick, and it's pouring rain—not to mention your hair! As you contemplate how you'll manage to muddle through work while your mind wanders and your stomach churns, we encourage you to think, *first things first*. By that we mean the skill of intense focus using three key questions: What is required for me right now to do the best job I can do? What did this audience come for? What does this audience need? Keep your answers uppermost in your mind, and you'll be ready-set-go on even the worst of days.

Confirm Your Tools and Your Territory

Nobody cares as much about your presentation as you do. Nobody. Likewise, no one cares about how bad your day has begun either! If you have to talk it out with someone, then give the details to a trusted friend—later. On your way to the office or event site, check with the administrative assistant, the maintenance person, or the security guard who can help you the most. Ask him or her if the room is unlocked and set up correctly. Ask for help in aligning the projector, the coffeemaker, and the lighting. If that is not possible, then let yourself know that it is not possible and focus on what you *can* do, preparing your three main points for the presentation.

Check the basics off your list, and you'll be in a better spot to think about content and process. In our experience, there is almost always one detail that you will overlook when you are frenzied or just plain having a bad day. An oversight is normal, just be ready for something like that so it does not surprise you.

In addition, you will receive great cooperation from others if you don't reveal too much about your inner emotional state. Consider saying simply, "I need your help. Would you be willing to help by—?" Whether you say this to a friend or an audiovisual person or the hotel manager, everyone will respond with a big smiling yes. When we let our anxiety speak, it comes across as either weak or as aggressive—neither is a good stance for them or for you.

The fact of the matter is that you know your stuff, and once the presentation has begun, it will have a life of its own. It's the little things that will unnerve you, so take care of those first. Be polite and understanding, never try to offload your anxiety on the security guy. Remember, what goes around, comes around!

With speakers at all levels of power and authority, small things can diminish their power. Presidents use microphones that don't work; VPs are missing a key handout; team leaders don't have enough chairs to seat their teams. Don't allow your power to be usurped by chairs and microphones and printers. This is your meeting, and you can have it your way so long as you show up early enough to make sure everything is prepared as you need it. Early preparation is positive prevention.

Write the Basics on a Half Sheet of Paper

If you focus on the core of your presentation, you'll stay on track. Allow that core to permeate your addled brain. Infuse it into your thoughts, so that if you're distracted up until and during the talk, your subconscious mind will take you back to your "through-line." The core of your presentation is very simply the three things you want your audience to know by the end of your presentation. It can and should be the opening meat of your presentation, the first things out of your mouth. This will make the audience sit up and listen. You will be *worth* listening to—and valued.

Write the main idea of your talk at the top of a half sheet of paper or a notepad sheet, for example, "Cohesion during this change," or "Connection not Perfection." Then list three points that you will stress throughout. Review your main idea on your way to the meeting. As you calm down and enter the area where you'll speak, you can gradually add in more detail. Don't make the mistake of reviewing your PowerPoint, because you'll forget the essence of your message. Once you begin and once your PowerPoint is in flow, you know what to do and say. The best presenters know "beyond and behind" the PowerPoint—they tell a story that links their slides. Without scaring yourself, you can even imagine that your PowerPoint breaks down and that all you have is the half sheet of paper to present with. That exercise will keep you focused on the essential. Imagining a useless PowerPoint or broken projector is an excellent way to boost your confidence by helping you focus on what is really important. The audience did not come to see your PowerPoint—they came to hear you.

Don't Be Too Hard on Yourself

Women in particular are prone to self-blame when things go wrong. They attribute any problems to their own lack of power, knowledge, personality, initiative, or talent—which is almost never the case. Don't think perfection; think connection. Even though you're having a bad day, be your real self—your best real self. Don't blame yourself if little things happen in ways you have not planned.

Never apologize. Ever. Don't apologize for anything that isn't immediately obvious to your listeners. Most of the time they are so concerned with themselves that they have no clue what may be happening unexpectedly for you. And after the presentation, leave the negatives at work. Don't take them home with you until you can discuss them with a mentor or a loved one as part of conversation—not in a rant. We learn more from conversations than from rants. Rants definitely feel better; they just don't make us better.

When having a bad-hair day on a presentation day,

- Ask for help with the details if you can. If you have no help, do what you can do, letting go of what is beyond you, and you'll feel that all is in order to the best of your ability. Don't get so attached to the little things you know will make a big difference, but only to you—chairs in alignment, space to walk, position of the microphone, and so forth. Time is always an issue on these days, so do what you can in the time that you have.

- Focus on the essence of your presentation. The essence is in your memory and in your expertise; you need no notes to talk about it. Knowing the essence will transition you through initial nervousness, past a bad attitude, and into helping the audience.

- Allow yourself mistakes and move forward with the advice of supporters. Think connection—not perfection—all the time, but especially on a bad-hair day. Chances are you will be pleasantly surprised at the positive outcome and so will your audience, who will know nothing about what went before!

Find quick and clever ways to establish rapport (these will vary with different audiences); after all your topic is unique, you are unique, and so is your audience. There is certainly no pat solution that will work for every speaker, but when you can combine humor and sincerity, you have taken the first and most important steps in connecting with your listeners. Second, look to your core competency and stay there. Third, and perhaps most important, respect the audience; no audience wants to be talked down to.

Jane Jackson Esparza
Cofounder and President
Cornerstone Speakers, LLC

15

Learn the Limits of Your Office Culture

Some of you reading this book have changed jobs a few times. (In fact, we now average about seven to thirteen jobs in a lifetime.) Others of you are beginning your career—in a meaningful job, on the right track to fulfilling your goals. No matter the point you're at in your career, take a moment to consider all the jobs you've held in your life.

As you think back on your work history, consider this: Wasn't each job different in its own particular way? Wasn't the culture of each organization at each job different again in a most particular way? Many of your coworkers have experienced several organizational cultures by the time they are thirty-five. While we learn a great deal from our own experience, we can learn from other people's experiences as well—and how to adapt to the people and the culture of the workspace.

When you speak and present as a member of the organization, keep in mind the particular culture of the company. Some companies are very relaxed and will want you to present while sitting down, others are more formal, some will even have an unspoken rule that the presenter dresses up for the occasion. Knowing the rules and customs—especially the unspoken ones—is important, no matter how much experience you have with other office cultures. What is vital is that you listen and adjust your antenna for culture signs that can help you and help your audience.

If you are coming from the outside or you are presenting at the home office in another city, you as the speaker must keep culture in mind at all times. Culture is important because it is unique, unspoken, and often neither written nor recorded. Every organization has a distinct flair, its cultural hallmark.

To better understand how culture is created, think of the first culture you experience in life—your family's. This unspoken part of our family dynamic adds a clear influence in our lives. Step over the line of what is okay in a family culture, and you will know—from the jokes you'll hear to the disapproval you'll encounter, you're clued in. Likewise, a corporate culture is also a usual part of every organization—though often not discussed or brought forth by anyone other than human resources. To say we are without a culture is like saying we are without air. Culture is all around us, and its emotional impact is important and significant.

The culture of an organization must be clearly grasped—especially by women, who are often left out of inner circle discussions and networks in traditional organizational cultures. A woman told Kevin that to network, she plays golf with the men in her organization, yet, of course, when they head to the locker room, she waits at the nineteenth hole—never privy to their conversation. If you work with many men, know that you are going to be out of the loop when the conversations gravitate to the locker room, the bathroom, or at the bar late at night. It is very useful, therefore to craft your relationships with the men in your organization in such a way that you will know what is going on, to whom it is happening, and when. While this will be informal conversation for the men, it will need to be more formalized for you through updates, clear questions, and male subordinates who will clue you in.

Being a temporary visitor or pretending to be one as an observer is one of the best ways to decipher culture. There is an old Polish saying: "The guest sees more in a day than the host sees in a month." As an insider or as an outsider, you can identify the cultural essentials of every audience you have by asking some basic questions like these:

- What is the educational and economic level of this group?

- How would you describe the morale and turnover of this group?

- How often does the group get together during off-work time?

- Are they more creative or analytical?

- Are they committed or just passing through?

- Do they respect each other?

And as you ask those questions, keep in mind that culture is very personal to people. Rarely will people comment on culture without emotion. Ask a friend about her company, and you'll notice immediately whether she likes it or not. She will probably say something like, "It's a great company." And if you probe respectfully, you will uncover culture. She may add, "Well, the people are so friendly and the managers are supportive." Or, "You can do anything you want, and nobody cares as long as you get your work done." Do you begin to decipher culture here? Creative? Free? Looser management? High self-esteem?

On the other hand, she may say, "Ugh, it's awful but I need the money." Again, if you ask why, she may say, "It's boring, humdrum, and there's no room to grow," or "It's so competitive. Nobody helps you out." Are you beginning to get a feel for the emotion that surrounds culture?

Don't be afraid to ask! And don't be afraid to ask many people to establish the majority of feelings about a particular company culture. Never, ever appear to be condescending or all-knowing about anyone else's workplace. You'll just end up being surprised, with your ego deflated. As we work with many companies, even those in the same industry, such as pharmaceuticals, we uncover the differences by interviewing ten to twelve team members. Within a short time, we learn the intimacies of culture, and we carefully attempt to understand where they work, live, and find meaning.

Every hospital, school, law firm, association, manufacturing facility, and telecom company is different. You can shine as a team member and as a presenter if you can communicate and connect with them about what makes them unique. As a woman, you are naturally good at this; women can tie pieces of information together and quilt them into a meaningful pattern.

To capture and maintain that grip on culture,

- Set yourself up for success by observing and asking insightful questions that decipher the aspects of the culture that are not written down. Start people talking about what is tacitly understood.

- Never criticize culture or attempt to be all-knowing. Appreciate differences, and learn from all sides of the issues. As a team member and as a presenter (as well as a future leader), you'll find your opinions are best shared after you hear and understand the others involved.

- Often it is easier for you, the outsider, to encourage dialogue about culture than it is for someone who works within that culture daily. Take advantage of any facilitating position you may occupy, so you can ask questions.

Knowing your audience is very important. I speak to numerous physician groups and many are composed primarily of men. As a young woman, I make sure that I engage my audience and know the data that I am presenting. I have to sell the audience with energy and interest in order to show that I am confident and knowledgeable about my content. With hecklers, do your job, do what you can do, focus and re-focus on the message you came to give.

Tammy Bratton, PharmD
Director, Regional Medical Liaisons
Amgen, Inc.

16

Adapt to the Expectations of Other Cultures

Contrary to what many books and lectures will tell you, you do not have to be an expert in cultural manners to be successful in today's business world. You need only be curious, respectful, and open. Too often being culturally attuned has meant reading books and pamphlets with the thought that somehow by memorizing a greeting or a way of eating you will assimilate into another culture. That is rarely the case. While many business people travel the world widely, some of us will stick close to home.

Regardless of your travel, however, it is increasingly evident that teams in the workplace will be multicultural. In the United States it has become very common to have a bevy of languages, cultures, and religions represented on one team working on projects that include others the world over. Even if you never set foot outside your hometown for business, you will be wise to consider yourself a world traveler on your team. Teams are now commonly composed of Caucasian, Latino, African-American, Muslim, Hindu, Chinese, Pakistani, Czech, Slovak, and Native American members.

You cannot be an expert in every subtlety of every religion or nationality. You can be an inquisitive "traveler" however—open, interested, accepting. This is even more helpful when you do the same with those who are from different regions of the United States. Texans do see the world a bit differently from their compatriots in Minnesota. California is different from New York or Chicago. Wichita Falls and Wichita are two very different places. Be sure to be interested, open, and accepting. Just because you are from the United States does not mean you are an expert. Take people's heritage and geography seriously. They do and they will remember that you did so. Respect others vigilantly.

Be a curious and interested listener rather than a quick-study expert when you are in a new place. You are more likely to be welcomed into the minds and hearts of others who are the true experts when you listen, ask good questions, and then share experiences from your own culture. This is especially important for the female presenter, because women are treated with varying degrees of respect, depending on where you travel. While gender biases are not so extreme in most countries as they were a generation ago, they still exist. Choose conservatively and tentatively rather than boldly and with risk. This applies to your travels in the United States as well. Deplane at LaGuardia in New York, and you are likely to see men in suits and ties, while in Los Angeles, a suit and tie make you feel like a stranger. The same is evident with local customs. You may find that New York is more egalitarian with men and women on teams, where the South still treats women with deference, and sometimes paternalistically. Don't be too quick to judge. Take your time to figure out how to adapt without giving in or being treated as less than you wish.

One valuable skill to utilize that will always work in your favor is respectful paraphrasing. When you have difficulty understanding an accent or a custom, simply rephrase or even repeat the content back to the speaker. "So the king of Thailand is a king for life," Kevin said to his host. "Oh, yes, here is his picture when he became king, and look over here, this is his most recent picture, sixty years later! Now let me show you . . . ," and on went the evening. Kevin knew nothing of his host's homeland, so he was full of questions and interest and became educated about a culture far away from his own. The two spoke of monks and women and children and men, industry and cars, history and the future. The key, of course, is curiosity and interest without passing judgment.

It is completely normal to make a mistake at a dinner, upon entering a home, or handing over a business card, even in the United States. When we engage in any new activity, we should do so with respectful curiosity. For example, one of Kevin's students from Kenya was telling him how uncomfortable it was for her to ask questions of her professor. "It is seen as a sign of disrespect in my culture— we don't want to offend our elders by questioning them," she said. Kevin, in this case, was the "elder" and he said, "I am so glad you told me that. In my culture, questions are welcomed and valued. How can you and I bridge our two cultures so that you feel comfortable?" Through a bit of back and forth, they arrived at a solution that suited them both, with each adopting new behaviors to experiment with. One interesting note here was that the student had a green card, which allowed her permanent residency in the United States, spoke flawless English, and had been in the United States for many years. Old customs never die; they simply need to be discussed with respect.

When you are immersed in a new culture,

- Show genuine interest in others. You will engage the part of them that encourages them to want to share with you. This is the continuing basis of relationship building that is so vital for your success in business and in the world today.

- Focus on the other person, and be careful not to come across as an expert. Instead, be seen as open and willing to learn. Watch your natural prejudices. We all have them. Information and connection with others will help dilute them.

- Encourage through understanding, never through judgment. Take every opportunity you can to learn from friends, seatmates on airplanes, next-door neighbors, and cube mates. The more you know, the more you can lead.

There is an old French saying: When you put your foot in the door, you had better put it in the right way or they will see your weakness and then you are dead. When preparing, I think about who is going to be there. I want to interest them, I want to respond and answer their questions. So I make sure I am not too scientific for the marketing audiences and not too general for the scientific ones.

Marie-Chantal Simard, PhD
Regional Medical Advisor
Medical Affairs
Abbott
Montreal

PART 3

Influence with Impact

17

Preparation Is the Key

We watched a scientist prepare for an important presentation. She was very bright, highly regarded, and extremely competent. In fact, she was "the" person in her field of expertise. She was a renowned expert about to address two hundred colleagues.

She worked on her slide deck over and over again, memorizing, moving slides, frowning, smiling, editing, and re-memorizing. She looked at her supporting materials and made sure of her footnotes. When we asked what she was doing, she looked up anxiously and said, "preparing."

Yes, she was "preparing," all right. She was preparing to be a sitting duck for what would become an ordinary, boring, lifeless, and therefore undistinguished presentation. In short, she was about to present one of those scientific treatises where people wouldn't remember what *she really wanted* them to remember—only what *they* wanted to. Despite her expertise, she ended up losing control of both the message and her audience.

An outstanding presentation depends on the presenter's ability to move away from the slides and data. Data is vital only in the context of the essential message you want to convey. Data feeds the essential message. It is not the essence itself.

Anyone who has heard a scientist, teacher, engineer, or physician present "their slides" knows that some presenters will kill your inquiring spirit with boredom, plainness, and an overall lack of energy. Kevin once asked a fellow audience member during a particularly dull lecture on the endo-cannabinoid system of the body how it was for him. The physician, continuing to look at the screen, said straight-faced, "Well, I am a physician. I have been trained to appear inter-ested." Your audiences need not cope in the same way, ever.

Other presenters bring the data to life and interest you in ways you never thought possible. For example, an oncology expert once began his presentation with a verbal descrip-tion of the pain as his patients had described it to him: "Like a locomotive racing down my throat . . . a wall of fire with each swallow . . ." His audience was primed to pay atten-tion to the positive effects of the treatment that he went on to explain, because he brought life to his presentation from the get-go. He knew that fellow physicians like the P-word—patients. They are whom they treat, the reason why they en-gage in the science, and their common bond. He knew and used the essence that bound them together right from the first words out of his mouth. You can, too.

The lesson? Present the essence of your message first. You do this best by preparing without your slides. Slides sup-port your message, but they are not your message—nor are they you. Your audience came to see and hear you.

Even the most experienced presenters make the mistake of letting their essential message be overshadowed by hard, cold data. The message must always be the essence, or core, of your presentation. That is the message you give when your projector fails. That is the message you relay to your partner at breakfast in a condensed form. That is the real reason you are there, and that is what your audience wants to hear.

As a woman, being able to distill the essence of your mes-sage is especially important because you are confronted with a variety of potential setbacks, including a higher voice, a slighter frame, and stereotypes that men in your audience may have about women. Like it or not, a good female presenter has to dismantle all the stereotypes by being completely on-point with her message and responsive in a warm way to her audience. Essentially, a female presenter has to send three messages very clearly: I know my stuff, I'm going to help you learn some very important stuff also, and I am an approachable teacher. When the female presenter does that, she towers over any competition. When she does only one thing well to the exclusion of the others, she becomes seen as arrogant, authoritarian, or weak. Combine the three, and you have intellectual acumen, congruent connection, and servant leadership.

How to prepare your essential message:

- Don't prepare your slides before you prepare your essential message. Essential messages are never on a slide—they are the wisdom coming from your mouth, your body, and the twinkle in your eye.

- Never confuse your data with the experience of you. Data on a slide should always support your essential or core message. The audience came to be with you, not with your data.

- Knowledge is of little value without action that converts data into wisdom, which is *targeted* knowledge. Your audience is waiting to be inspired. They want to do something with what they are learning. Regardless of their technical expertise, their cognitive training, their degrees, or their age, they want to learn and act on what they have just learned from you. In short, they want to be turned on to your data. That is what we mean by wisdom.

Know the one key thing you want to leave them with. Write it down and have it in hand. Tell yourself, don't forget this! Often, you'll prepare and then somehow in being nervous or inexperi-enced, you will forget the one key thing you wanted to say. Actually articulate it in writing ahead of time.

> Adrienne Antink, CAE
> VP Component Relations
> Medical Group Management
>   Association

18

Assert Your Authority

We know a female presenter who is quite knowledgeable in the field of international etiquette. She is an established author and global traveler; she consults with business and industry on global protocol. Yet we have watched this very expert lose her credibility in front of an audience by responding with more information than necessary. When asked how she entered the field, she replied, "Well, as a young woman, I married a German businessman and had to learn protocol by going to all the receptions as his wife. When we got divorced, I thought, *I'll do something with this*, and so I turned it into a business."

Her girlfriends might appreciate knowing every nuance of her success; however, a more powerful business response would simply have been, "I lived abroad as a young woman and began to learn the culture at receptions and events. This was the impetus for my business."

Every one of us has to make choices with just how much we reveal about ourselves and when we do so. There is nothing wrong with our friend revealing her divorce; in fact, it was the divorce that propelled her into her work. However, there are many ways to inform others not only of what they need to know, but also what they want to know.

As you work on the core or essential message of your presentation, be prepared to say the same thing about yourself through normal conversation. When someone says, "Tell me about yourself," they are not really asking for every detail. What they are really asking is, "Tell me something about you so that I can link it with something about me so I can feel more comfortable talking to you about me and maybe even us!" TMI (too much information) can be a useful inner watchword for every rising executive. As flattering as it might appear, most people are not all that interested in you; they want to talk about themselves. If you want to be influential, you'll want to focus on them also. When you listen well, you will be regarded as a great conversationalist even though mostly you'll be asking and listening, rarely self-disclosing. It is a paradox that plays itself out daily; listen well, and others think you are smart, savvy, and very special. In fact, there are so few really good listeners in the world, especially as you move higher in an organization; you will likely distinguish yourself with this one key skill. Show genuine interest, and listen.

Therefore, when speaking to anyone at work or at play, consider who your target is and what they are really asking of you, and then decide if they need or want to know about your divorce, the traffic jam today, your plane delay, or your kids. Be strategic about your choice-making.

Recognize That the Expert Is You

When you speak, your confidence, your experience, and your expertise should always shine through. Be certain to give the audience your position on the topic without apology. Even if you don't have years of experience behind you, you have a unique perspective. We know a young female speaker who looks like a freckled thirteen-year-old and who commands a nice six-figure salary as a sales trainer. While young in age and in appearance, she has lessons to teach us all; she is an expert in her field. No matter your experience, speak with firm words such as, "I have found that . . ." or "In my experience, this is the case because" rather than tentative language such as, "I know this is kind of hard to, you know, relate to, but I guess I think . . ."

In college you could use the word *like* in almost every sentence without worry or regard. In some instances, it was cute and even charming. In the world of work, *like* is a career buster. Now is the time to sprinkle more decisive words such as *yes, no, determine, decide, conclude, will, aim, on track, my honor to, I understand, help me understand, let's,* and the ever-useful *thank you.* Contrast that language with what we refer to as pathetic language for any business situation where you want to have influence. Avoid words such as *but, wish, hope, maybe, problem, disagree, wrong, try, should, maybe, frankly, have to, got to, basically, totally, to tell you the truth, I have to be honest with you,* and, of course, the ever-annoying *like.* As a woman, make sure you don't use weak-sounding words. In like manner, we are not advocating being tough. We are suggesting sounding decisive, authoritative, and knowledgeable. Words matter.

Learn to quote yourself rather than others. Sure, it's fine to unify your presentation around a classic quote, but back it up with your own opinions. If you quote too many other people—authors, researchers, poets, scholars—it only encourages the audience to read someone else's work or think of them, when you really want to be the one who is top of mind. Too many quotes by others tends to weaken *your* message. Use others' quotes only to support the "show," which is you.

Avoid also the common and amateurish use of cartoons in your slide deck. If you must use a cartoon, remove the text, show the picture, and speak aloud the caption for the cartoon. That allows everyone to get the joke, directs the attention to you, and permits the cartoon to again support your message rather than be your message. Few speakers use cartoons well. We suggest you avoid doing so until you perfect it as a technique. You don't need to be funny to give a successful presentation. You do need to respond warmly to any natural humor that comes from the audience or from you. Jokes, cartoons, or Internet missives are traps you do not want to step into. Remember, they came to hear *you*!

Don't Use Soft Examples

Too many women fall into the trap of using personal examples about their children and family to illustrate points. We have heard women with more than thirty years' experience address highly technical audiences using examples about their sons' driving and their hairstylist's names. This hurts their credibility with both women and men. Certainly, a well-timed perspective from a child can work, but it must be very, very well timed—after you have already built your authority with the audience. Consider this: How many executive men talk about their families or the funny things their children did at playtime?

Your examples should center on the competition, the product, relevant past history, what specific segments of your industry are doing, or what you have learned from past experiences with the topic. Short stories are great so long as they have a relevant point. Use statistics, definitions, and "hard" examples. You can temper them with emotion and examples from home so long as they are not your lead examples. Be known for your attention to data, knowledge, research, and mostly for your commonsense wisdom. If you choose to go toward a softer example, use a male team member to join in the story. "Bob and I were sharing stories of our dogs the other day, and he said something very useful" is better than, "Daisy, my Rottweiler, did the cutest thing yesterday." Always follow up these personal examples with the punch line that is the teaching point for the audience. "The point is . . . The reason this is important . . . What I learned was . . ." will help lead the audience back to your message even if they hated or endured your message about home, family, pets, or your latest vacation. When it comes to personal information, use it but remember that less is more.

The audience can relate your examples to what is going on in their own lives without you having to use a "too personal" personal anecdote. After one of our seminars, a middle-aged woman approached us to say that she thought of her teenaged daughter during the whole section on conflict. We did not mention anything about family conflict during the presentation; the woman made sense of it in her own personal way. Audiences learn beyond us and sometimes in spite of us!

Women Are Natural Experts

Be comfortable with your expertise. Too many women are trained to be modest and unassuming about the very things they should be clearly communicating to help others succeed. Take command of what you do best. Be confident, don't be apologetic, target your message, and understand your unique value. Help others see *that* you know and *what* you know.

If you truly appreciate or even like most men—that is, if you find them approachable—it shows through because you don't put them on the defensive. You see men as equals—different but interesting and part of the whole scenario of work and life. You wouldn't want to work without them, just as you are not totally dependent upon them for your thoughts and opinions. Many men, like many women, enjoy being enjoyed. Reach out to them in a professional, friendly way. Be careful not to send sexual or seductive signals while doing so. Such behavior, however innocent, may get men to turn their heads at the clubs, but it will not benefit you at work. Be known for your substance, your expertise, your friendliness and interest, not for batting your eyes or revealing too much skin. You will undoubtedly see women use their femaleness in ways that are seductive, sometimes innocently. They are undermining their credibility each and every time they do so. Some will get promoted, yet always at an expense to themselves. This type of promotion rarely leads in the direction they intend.

Some women are suspicious of men, often stemming from a situation at home or a job in the past. One woman we coached summed her experience up by saying, "The men in my department are like children, and I am their babysitter. They don't think they need me till they need me." Needless to say, she was stuck in a rut in her career, embittered and angry. The strain showed on her face and in her attitude. She thought that she was limited by the men. She was really limited by herself.

To show your expertise,

- Own it. Don't apologize for it. People will trust you more because of this that assertiveness.

- Exemplify it. Don't dig up family memories when you don't need to. You have relevant examples everywhere because you live them every day on the job.

- Be it. Enjoy being a female who knows a lot. Enjoy the males in your audiences, and acknowledge that, together, you make the world of work exciting and interesting.

I never go into a presentation or meeting focused on a person's title; I take the same approach with a CEO as I would with an assistant to a media director. Everyone's important at the end of

*the day, and deserves the same respect and preparation for a
meeting.*

> Kristin MacGregor
> Account Executive
> Advertising Sales
> Google

19

Be an Effective Teacher and Facilitator

The fundamental task of the presenter is to teach. A wedding toast, a eulogy, a ten-minute update, or a two-hour presentation is meant to convey, to foster learning, to *teach*. The presenter must therefore create an environment for learning. When we engage another adult in the learning process, there are times when he or she needs what we have: a new data-entry system, a way to develop a team, statistical formulas, how to get the budget approved. Those activities, at least at first, require that the teacher give the learner what the teacher has and what the learner does not yet have—the essential building blocks of the skill or knowledge.

But being a teacher is more than being a giver; it also requires the skill of being the encourager and the initiator of the conversation—being a facilitator. In the past decade we have noticed that it is the presenter who is also skilled at being an expert facilitator who can make the greatest impact on productivity, with influence and, ultimately, with leadership.

The word *education* comes from the Latin *educare* which literally means "to draw forth from." It does not mean "to dump into." This is an important distinction for your effectiveness as a presenter. Remember those college professors who lectured for hours on end, no questions taken, using old notes from past years, droning on and on? As they "gave" the data to you, so, too, did you regurgitate the information on test day to promptly forget it all. That may not have happened every time, especially if the material was in your major or was vital or relevant to you personally. But often those kinds of lifeless lectures were an old style of teaching. In essence, that style makes the professor a repository and the student a vessel. The professor fills the student.

Those professors who were more Socratic in their methods, asking you questions, drawing forth your experiences and understanding your point of view, were a bit closer demonstrating what will be expected of you in the corporate world. The standard for presenters will be their ability to facilitate, to discuss, to prompt others, and to manage the discussion without losing focus or authority. That is how great teams are built.

Three Essential Messages

In a restaurant, we peruse the menu, confer with our friends and our waiter, and then make our choice. That is the activity of the first essential message, what we call "the put-in" or the "training for needed skills." Regardless of the skill being transferred, it requires the cooperation and the activity of the learner. Therefore, whenever you present any kind of data or content or skill, first be very aware that the learner is making choices beyond your control to "decide." Rather, they are deciding if and how they will learn the material.

Second, you should also understand what is important to learners and how to elicit those priorities from them. This is a "valuing activity" in the mind of the learner because it helps them distinguish what is important and what is not. Have you ever been given directions at a gas station only to forget them down the road? It is not that the material was not relevant; it was that you placed more importance on one part of the directions than on the other. What would have happened if the attendant had asked you to repeat the directions? What might have occurred if the attendant asked you how you remembered things best prior to giving you the directions? What would it have been like for you the last time you learned any skill or data point if you and the teacher had discussed what was important, why it was relevant, what it reminded you of—in short, what would have happened if they drew forth from you what you had to put into the learning?

Third, beyond understanding how learners choose and how to elicit their cooperation, we must also understand the value of encouragement in the educational process. Especially for the female presenter, that can be a vital insight. Most men like women to ask them questions. Why? Men like to be affirmed and encouraged, especially by women. And men like to have their ideas or at least their good intentions validated—again, especially by female colleagues. That is not to say that your fellow females do not appreciate validation, it is simply that men certainly do. Remember your first date? Who did more talking about themselves?

The Female Advantage

When the female presenter begins by "drawing forth" instead of "dumping into" she has a tremendous advantage—the change advantage. Men and women are much more likely to change and to move when they first feel understood. The best way to accomplish that is to demonstrate from the beginning that you do understand or that you want to understand. Understanding comes first, agreement later. Agreement is a different matter and may take more time. Understanding is a skill many women possess based on culture, innate skill, and family training. Many men have been told from day one to "know, decide, and do," and whether they are good at it or not, that is what they innately move toward. That is why women tend to nurture one another without necessarily jumping into advice and solutions, whereas men feel more comfortable going right to "here is what you should do." It isn't true for all of us. It is true for some, and if you are on the lookout for it, you will find that tendency easier to deal with.

What this understanding piece does for the learner is to reassure them that they are okay and that they are included and connected—the hallmark of any learning process. Thus, the first task of the presenter is one of listening and understanding. That does not mean you begin your presentation with a discussion or even with a question. You, as the presenter, need to set the context, the content, the task, and the tone of the meeting. You could conduct some short phone preinterviews with selected audience members, asking what they most want from the meeting. Listening here will change the entire character of your meeting. Attendees want to come and hear their own concerns being addressed—what could be better?

You are at the peak of your teaching, however, when you stimulate thought in the learner. That can be done with presentations of all kinds so long as you remember that questions stimulate more thought than data, facts, and opinions do. Great presenters who know how to prompt our thinking actually turn over the majority of the learning enterprise to us early and often in their presentations. When you present to your next audience, focus your early remarks so that it shows you understand what they understand to be true. That will start them nodding their heads in agreement with your assessment. Then ask the question. The question encourages their thinking and not just their recall. And by encouraging their thinking, you will be demonstrating your highest value to them. Make sure this question is an open question, one that cannot be answered with a simple yes or no. Some presenters find it useful to write the question down ahead of time so that they are not tempted to ask a closed-ended question, which can be answered briefly and without much thought. You can highlight the question on a PowerPoint slide if you wish.

You can have enormous influence with others—allowing them to do what they are going to do anyway: think and decide if you are worth listening to!

Stay aware of the following:

- There are many ways to learn. Few are related to your lecture. What happens in the learner's head during your lecture and perhaps between you and this person is the real learning. Open yourself to questions that help the learner figure things out, and it will help you figure out what they are figuring out! That interaction is vital for you to gauge their future cooperation.

- Don't feel threatened when you don't know an answer. React with some glee to the journey you can both take together into the unknown. If you are supposed to know the answer and you don't, simply solicit it from someone else. Become the teacher, facilitator, and ring mistress (yes, Ringling Bros. Circus has one), and help get the flow of information going. You can even say with a hint of mischief, "Before I give you what *I* think about that, I wonder what some of *you* think about that?"

- Every presenter teaches. When we are aware of our teaching role, we tend to work harder in crafting our message and celebrate hitting the target more intentionally. Make every presentation about them, the audience, not about you, the star. Your star will rise the more you look to them.

You can tell when people are comfortable; they welcome questions because they know the material; they are confident sharing their opinions and perspectives.

> Amy Huntington
> President
> Juno Lighting Group

20

Focus on the Essentials

We spend a considerable amount of time coaching speakers to "throw meat out to the audience" before they do anything else. It may sound carnivorous, but if you're a hungry audience member, you are craving the meat of the presentation first and foremost. Female speakers suffer a bad reputation for not reaching the essential meat of their presentation until the audience has already tuned out. There are the *thank-yous*, the *I'm sorry fors*, the unneeded *I hope yous*, and then—much too late—the main point. Adult audiences require the main points early on so that they can apply them mentally throughout the rest of your presentation. Equally important, they need to see that you know what you're talking about and that you are worthy to be heard. Therefore, both literally and figuratively, show your last slide first. Get to the heart of the discussion right away. This applies to a meeting of two thousand, for twenty, or a meeting just for two. Tell them what you are going to tell them early, right away, now!

Imagine you are a member of the audience. You are there to be inspired by an expert, to better understand information, or perhaps to be persuaded to buy something you will discover you need. Imagine you are the only one who knows that an evacuation is about to occur and your talk will have to abruptly end. You have only one minute before chaos breaks loose and you will lose your audience. What would you say? Try it right now. Think of the presentation you just gave or will give soon. What is your key message?

In order to hone your essential message, you must be able to articulate clearly and descriptively. Challenge yourself to use fewer words, but make those words count by choosing them carefully. Avoid jargon like *step up to the plate, game plan,* and words like *paradigm, matrix,* or *granular.* Enjoy the breadth of the language; use the thesaurus on your computer or your bookshelf. For example, there are at least six other words you can use instead of *goal, profit,* and *mission,* so that you can avoid repetition. More important, when your audience hears these new words, they have to make room in their heads to house these words. Use old, repetitive words, and you run the risk of them being stored with the last presenter, the terrible presenter, or the generic presenter. By making unique and varied language choices, you are putting a fresh and memorable spin on your presentation.

Consider taking a word that is common in your industry, focusing on it a bit, and then redefining it. *Granular* can mean "detailed"; it can also mean that every detail, every person is important. *Stepping up to the plate* can mean "individual responsibility"; it can also imply that I know my team is supporting me from the dugout and my coach is waiting for me as I round third base. Be creative in your use of words, and make your own functional meaning out of the most commonly used of them. When asked if he takes risks, Dr. Mehmood Khan, chief scientific officer at Pepsico said, "There is a difference between *risk* and *chance.* With risk, you can calculate the variables; with chance, you cannot. I do take risks, but I never leave them to chance." He defined his words and taught a great lesson.

The adult attention span is about seven to twelve minutes. Consider that fact as you prepare your presentation so that you have a better gauge for how long you should spend highlighting the essentials. Try using a seven-minute timer when you practice. You should reduce your main ideas to seven minutes. Your audience will love you for it.

That's not to say you give only a seven-minute talk! It does mean, however, that your main points might be best conveyed one at a time, in seven-minute segments. Perhaps also a one-hour presentation might have room for some discussion in small groups, interaction with you as the presenter, and so on. Be creative in your use of your time for the benefit of the audience, and you will be the memorable one.

To stay focused remember to,

- Think most about the audience and least about you. Overcome the tendency to worry about what you're wearing and whether you've memorized your note cards, and instead imagine yourself sitting in their seat. What would you want to hear? What is critical for you to understand?

- Edit your detail like you clean out your junk drawer. Be merciless. Anything that isn't essential must go. The audience won't remember it all anyway. Nobody appreciates your junk.

- Use new words. Challenge yourself to describe the mundane with intelligence. This helps grab and keep others attention. If you must use ordinary jargon, redefine it.

Less is more on slides . . . three bullet points at most . . . the rest is conveyed to them through me, not through my slides. I usually use eight slides for fifteen minutes of presentation.

Helen Torley, MD
VP and General Manager of the
Nephrology Business Unit
Amgen Corporation

21

Be an Astute Listener

Imagine you are asked to facilitate or moderate a meeting or you are attending a team meeting with one person, your boss, or a team of others collaborating on a project. The real task of the presenter or the attendee is the same—to listen. Presenters listen to their audiences, and audience members listen also. Team members rise in value and status by listening. When you are an astute listener, you are focused on the target. You won't listen to everything, only to that which is necessary at this time and place, for this person and this agenda. Use this chapter to help you listen with that target in mind.

Isn't it interesting that most people aren't very good at it? Listening is a learned skill that many never really learn. We learn to talk. We even are sometimes required to take a speech course in high school or college. Rarely are we required to take a listening course. Women have an edge here. Women have proved to be better listeners in most research studies. Women traditionally are more able to discern emotional meaning in messages than are men. Women can also paraphrase and summarize more naturally. Men who are trained in counseling and related fields learn to listen with those same skills. In all fairness, there are men who listen extremely well and women who do not. When you're asked to present in front of a group, tap into your listening ability.

That means to tap into what others need to link your knowledge with their own to achieve your mutual goal. That is leadership. Leadership begins with listening.

Listening Has Many Levels

The most basic level is to listen and paraphrase back information. At that level, you are not evaluating or analyzing or projecting the information forward. You are simply homing in on the essence of the factual piece of the communication. An example of paraphrasing is, "So you're saying that the role of senior executive director has many hidden expectations."

This is not as simple as it may look. You have to let go of your opinions here. Using their words to get to the essence of what they are saying is the key. Don't interpret, don't judge, and don't even use an alternative word. Get as close to their meaning without "parroting" their words, and you will have it. They will respond by saying more than yes. Often when you are accurate with a paraphrase, especially when it has some urgency or importance to it, you will hear them say, "Absolutely!" It is not at all uncommon for them to then expand on what they said with even more detail. When that happens, what do you do next? You paraphrase!

The next level of listening checks your perception of how the other is feeling. An example might be, "You're frustrated because you're unclear about priorities as the newest senior director." Touching base is helpful because you will sometimes hear an emotion that they thought was flying under the radar as undetectable. So, say what you hear, and be ready for a reaction from them. When you tap the emotion with the paraphrase, you are using empathy. Many use paraphrasing and empathy with a question mark at the end. "Are you saying you are wondering if you are up to this new job?" You can do that. A more effective form is with a period at the end. Rather than question, just state what you hear. It will have more impact. "You wonder if you are up to this new job." Experiment, and you'll notice the difference immediately in the quality of their response.

Level Your Awareness

A skilled team member and facilitator is always aware of the potential for conflict to take over what could be a healthy discussion. Whether you are a leader or a member of the team, always consider yourself a leader. We teach the concept of leveled awareness every time we work with leaders who need to manage conflict. Leveled awareness simply means nonstop observation of what, why, and how conflict erupts in the group. Psychologists call this being "psychologically minded." Those using this skill pay attention on three levels at once, and then they unify, or level, them. On the one level is what is being said, on the other is what is being felt, still on another is what is being left unsaid.

Women are typically very astute at leveling awareness. They use their skills of perception—nonverbally and instinctively—to acknowledge the level of disagreement before them. The key for the moderator or facilitator is to share that awareness with the group.

For example, you might say,

> - "I sense an opportunity to stop and discuss what just happened."
>
> - "Obviously there are strong feelings about this. Let's go around and let each of you make a statement."

The group needs you to do this. They are each involved in their own reaction and less inclined to doing anything about it to find a solution. You can do this as a participant as well. Be aware always of the target or goal in mind. Be careful not to be too sensitive. If need be, wait and see what plays out. Being the first to wade into the fray is not always wise. Build support gradually by, as much as possible, bringing the many sides together to focus on common ground.

Another very effective listening technique you can use as a team member is to summarize what others on the team have said. Keep it focused, concise, and to the point. It is remarkable how you can impact the direction of discussion if you summarize every fifteen to twenty minutes throughout a meeting. Summarizing causes all to listen better as the meeting continues.

Therefore, when you want to prove yourself as an astute listener, remember:

- Paraphrasing and summarizing cannot be done without listening. Never assume. Check it out with a good paraphrase. It will build rapport and increase your credibility.

- Listening cannot be done without awareness. Tune in to find out what is being said and felt, as well as what is *not* being said.

- If you become aware of something that is emotionally charged or controversial, build support before you introduce the topic.

I am increasingly less interested in my opinion as I am in theirs.
Olympia Dukakis
Academy Award–winning actress and director

22

The Audiovisual Conundrum

In 1964, cultural researcher Marshall McLuhan talked about the medium as the message. He asserted that how we communicated the message said more than what was being communicated. While he was referring to the onslaught of the television age upon society, we can apply his thinking to today's onslaught of computer visuals upon the unsuspecting presenter and the audience.

Today's corporate attendees are in a state of PowerPoint paralysis. While it is the state of the art, PowerPoint is routinely misused because we don't stop to think about a key question: What is the very best way to convey this message?

You Rule—Not the Visual

As coaches, we've observed an overarching problem: the annoying overuse of PowerPoint. The truth is that your presentations will never be effective if you are communicating your message using complicated audiovisual tools that you don't know how to use properly. Even if you are a Power-Point expert, it is important for you to get back to basics and relearn the essential elements of a great presentation, which include making eye contact and interacting with your audience.

Do a self-check right now. Are you guilty of letting your software rule your presentations? Do you—

- Write your speech using the PowerPoint software?

- Edit your slides five minutes before walking on?

- Feel panic if you can't find your laser pointer?

- Feel deathly ill if the projector is broken?

- Have no idea what eye contact is or means?

- Feel unequivocally powerful as you flip from slide to slide?

- Summon your personal power from your PowerPoint?

If you can relate to most of these, it is time for you to break the PowerPoint habit.

PowerPoint Rehab

Your thoughts and your point of view are what the audience wants and needs. Many today in corporate life use their PowerPoint as the archive of all that is right about their topic. Then they use this archive as the presentation. Your archive is not your presentation. Archives live in files and libraries; presentations are organic and alive.

It is possible to break the habit. Begin by drafting your speech on paper or in a word-processing document. Erase, cross out, and think. Write paragraphs when you feel like it. Outline the key words of a story. Think again. Jot down a quote from Shakespeare or your mother-in-law. Let the thought process evolve without the lure of bullet points and without the reminder of layout, bar graphs, animation, and Insert Here commands.

This flexibility is especially important for the female speaker who wants to be noticed for her unique thinking and not for her data presentation alone. It is essential for women today to be perceived as a force to be reckoned with when it comes to thought, value, and anticipation of need for their teams and their bosses. When you have that kind of value, you will be needed by those around you and you'll be considered irreplaceable. Getting it right is only half the story; getting it heard—getting you heard—is the critical part. In corporate life today, many women are in support positions to men. Administrative professionals, meeting planning, marketing, and human resources are just a few of the places in corporate life where women are the majority. But what about the C-suite at your workplace? How many women are chief officers? If your sights are set on those offices for yourself, then begin to think as those who reside there do.

C-suite members are able to focus and are rarely distracted by details. Others do that for them. They don't always worry about everything, only the important things. They know whom they want to talk to, and they make time for them. As you look at how you use presentation technology, understand how your inner "you" is thinking. Are you working to be perfect or useful? Right or on track? Subordinate or self-confident? How you answer those questions may help you then shape not only what you will say but also how you will say it and with what technology. This frame of mind is what will make you a star presenter— unforgettable and useful.

On the other hand, if your presentations and your presentation style are generic, ordinary, and like everyone else's, then you become a commodity and, in effect, nonessential. Being sidelined in such a manner is not good for women who still have to compete and cope with lingering chauvinism. You don't want to be pegged as a commodity in your role because of ageism and sexism. Be seen for the real value you possess.

We've said it before, and here it is again—they came to see and hear *you*, not your slide deck.

Next, clarify your purpose—your essence—the "why" behind the talk. Only after that is clear in your mind should you go to the computer and the visual design. But as you work with the software, constantly imagine yourself speaking without it. Only then will it become secondary and not integral to your message.

Once you have the essence of your message and the main points you will use to support it, consider the visual theme you desire, and go into the program. Decide if the theme is enhanced, not enslaved, by the system, and how you will use your visuals to your advantage. Use words and sentences very sparingly on slides. You should do the talking, the audience should not be doing the reading. Use graphics and photos that illustrate the concept. Watch the overuse of redundant clip art. Most speakers have too many slides—not too few—so edit your images ruthlessly. You can always reproduce them on a handout, for the audience members to browse as you present—or even better, promise that you will e-mail them afterwards.

When you are in front of the audience, begin with a dynamic cover slide that accents you and your purpose and anchors the theme. Here, PowerPoint can be an effective backdrop, making you the star of the show. Then, as you present, use the B key to keep the audience focused on what you have to say, rather than on the bullet points. Simply press B for black screen, and there you have it—the slides fade to black and will provide you with an opportunity to discuss a point, emphasize a key item, or take a question. Simply hit the B key again to continue—it lets you pick up at the same slide you left off. Send a message that you are in charge of your presentation. What is amazing is that as soon as you black out the slide, the audience looks right at you! Magic!

Another piece of technology that works to your benefit is the remote mouse. The small handheld device wirelessly connected to your computer allows you to advance the slides. The remote mouse allows you to move all around the room as you speak. Presenters who don't use it are destined to stand next to their computer, manually advancing each slide, and perhaps looking stilted and amateurish. Don't take away from your movement and your credibility. Movement typically energizes both you and the audience and is a very effective strategy for most presenters.

Some remotes allow you to darken the screen just as the B key will. Again, when the screen goes dark, all eyes are on you, rather than on the slides. (If you want a white screen, just hit the w key!)

The point is to give yourself the freedom of movement.

People Like the Flipchart

When a speaker uses the flipchart (a large pad of paper on a stand-up easel) or the whiteboard (also known as a dry-erase board) to illustrate a point, people perk up. Consider using the flipchart or white board every time you present. Have a few ideas in mind that will work particularly well on a whiteboard. For example, a list or a simple drawing will accent almost any presentation, and both are easy to quickly jot down on a whiteboard or flipchart. Remember when you are writing to stop talking. Speak only when you can see the audience, never when you are looking away from them.

When you have filled a sheet of paper with ideas, rather than casting if off to the side, consider posting it on the wall. Some flipchart paper is manufactured as Post-it Notes and is postable without masking tape. The effect of poster paper on the walls is that of a real workshop. The audience is surrounded by their contributions; they are thinking, "Look what we did! Your presentation was different!"

We have seen this work beautifully with the most astoundingly technical presentations. A clean, clear black or blue marker works best. Avoid red. Purple and green are interesting, but not for every word. Write large, and use bullet points, check marks, or numbers to differentiate points. Use the flipchart proudly—never apologetically. It is an integral part of your presentation. What audiences like about it is that it is not PowerPoint, which they know has been prepared well in advance. Flipcharts give them a feeling of specialness and spontaneity. It allows you to be spontaneous also and to linger on a point worth talking about in more detail.

The flipchart conveys that you are thinking spontaneously, responding in real time, and valuing what your audience is saying and contributing—all great selling points to an audience. Audiences enjoy cocreating in the now with their presenter.

One last and vital piece of technical advice: Never use your laptop as your TelePrompTer. This is the mark of an unprepared presenter or a rank amateur. We call this the *Saturday Night Live* guest-host effect, since guest hosts on that television show rarely memorize their lines and are thus doomed to read from the TelePrompTer offstage. It is fine to look at the large screen to see where you are; just don't talk to the screen—and never to the laptop!

In technical presentations, remember:

- Your mind is much more important than any computer visual program. Let the audience share your thinking, question your ideas, argue and applaud your logic, and learn with you.

- Learn enough about the visual systems available to you to enhance your point but not enslave yourself. Simple and clear is always better than too many slides and redundancy. If someone or another department is pressuring you to use certain slides, do so, but with the savvy to move them through quickly and summarize the points. You may have to show the slide. You do not have to linger on it. Convey its message and move on.

- Take control. Darken the screen, move around the room, if you are unsure, use large note cards with your notes in very large print for security, ask questions, use the chart or board in the room, and enjoy your presentation. This enthusiasm will have a contagious effect on the audience, and they'll like your presentation more, too.

- Never, ever, never say, "I know you can't read this but . . ." If they can't read it, make it so that they can!

My advice to young women: Know your content so well that you don't stand behind the lectern with notes. Use your PowerPoint as a way to trigger your thoughts with only a few words on each slide.

> Gail Wolf
> Professor of Nursing Leadership
> University of Pittsburgh School of
> Nursing

23

Connect with the Decision Makers

In any enterprise, someone makes the big decisions. Their job is to think and strategize, to question and to look forward. Watch any committee at work, and you'll find that despite what they say about collegiality and consensus, there is always a pivotal person who engineers the decisions that are made, or who is always the key person in the decision-making process. Often that person pointedly questions, listens, waits, and then says something that turns heads. Those people are the leaders.

When you present, from the front of the room or from your seat within the room, figure out early on who the decision maker is. Your message, data, questions, and overall emphasis need to be tailored for that person. You don't need to "pander" to the decision maker. After all, we are not called upon simply to tell every decision maker what she or he wants to hear. We do need to understand that they are the direction setter, and therefore our work is to support their goal. One company CEO we work with writes his three to five goals for the year on a half sheet of paper. He passes it down to the next level, and their task is to write on a full sheet of paper the six to ten goals they have to support him. On and on it goes down the line, each level figuring out how to support the levels above. This is alignment and transparency. When you know what the boss and the boss's boss need to accomplish, you know full well what you have to do. You also will know what they need to know from you.

Words Can Get in the Way

Always know the key facts about the main decision maker. Know in advance by asking good questions of those closest to the person. Make very good friends with those "in the know." Associate yourself with those who are higher up in the organization than you are, people more experienced and more connected. Start with the administrative professional. She or he will tell you precisely what their executive wants. Run things past them for their review. Treat what they say as confidential, even if it is not. Never inquire about anything other than what applies to you, but keep an ear out for what you will hear anyway. Information is always helpful, even when not for public consumption. Be vigilant about keeping their confidences.

Information may be power, but the right information is powerfully transformative. Powerful presenters have sifted information. They listened to the many and chose from the few to better inform their message. Listening to the right people helps connect you to the right people. One CEO asked a different administrative assistant to accompany him to the airport each trip. It was his way of connecting with those he rarely saw. On the way, he was full of questions. The next week, there were always improvements to security, the parking lot, the food, e-mail, and so forth. Some wondered where he got all his good ideas. There was always one administrative professional quietly smiling as the change was rolled out. Sometimes the important people are at the top, sometimes they are in the middle, sometimes both!

Be seen as a collaborator—not as a rumormonger. Every interaction you have is a sacred confidence. Once you are known as a big mouth, your influence is severely limited—as will be your career. It is vital that in your work to find the decision maker you not come off as a "climber," someone who is only out for herself. They exist; just don't become one. Rather focus on the task, the process, the job—help others, and they will help you.

Find Value in Action

Your value for the decision maker rests with how well you can help her solve problems—real problems. Regardless of your academic background, age, or prior experience, you will be sought after when you are seen as a problem solver. The value here is that if you are seen as valuable, the decision maker actually comes to you! Therefore, in your meetings, whether you are the presenter or the team member, think about how to help, not only how to shine; think value, not only reward; think about solutions, not only about being the one who came up with them. Leaders have an eye for those who take action.

The first way to be of value is to listen not only to the problems of the organization, but also to the core problem for that particular person. Every senior executive in the organization has an issue that is of vital importance to him or her. It is their hot button, the issue that keeps them up at night. Know this, and you'll know them.

Our real value is drawing the end result forth from the client, the boss, and the colleague. When that happens, you are needed. Your value increases. The applause may be for the other person or the team at the end of the line, but the teacher will be you.

Therefore, when you are presenting,

- Be aware of who is who. Speak with the wisdom you gain from understanding the decision maker in your audience.

- Concern yourself with being of service, not with having all the answers. Become adept at asking in-depth questions. That is likely to be your greatest value.

- Allow the final applause for your client—the real decision maker.

We are not there to please the audience. We are there to engage them.

Nora Dunn
Actress, Comedienne, Director

24

Communicate with the C-suite

In most organizations, the C-suite is made up of the "chief" positions of leadership: the CEO (Chief Executive Officer), CFO (Chief Financial Officer), CLO (Chief Learning Officer), and the COO (Chief Operating Officer). Oftentimes, other top positions in marketing, human resources, sales, engineering, and communications are also members of the C-suite. Typically, the C-suite is male, but there are always exceptions in companies that are led by female CEOs. Our female clients tell us that overall parity is improving, but that women are still in the minority when it comes to the highest levels of power in the organization. That growing improvement is helpful, especially to a woman entering the organization. You may very well be in the C-suite sooner and faster than your female bosses could ever have dreamed possible.

Though it may seem as though the C-suite is a self-sufficient unit, often they have even more of a need to communicate and build their team than the rest of the organization does. They're not the first people who come to mind when the training department is looking for people to train, but often, they are so busy running the show that they have little time to step outside the box and take an honest look at how they are influencing the rest of the company.

If and when you are in a position to influence this group, we have one word to say: Go! If you've gotten this far, then you deserve it and you have probably already proved yourself to some extent among your bosses and peers. Your job is to demonstrate your value. Like every other audience, the C-suite wants the experience of you and your work—in short, you have something they want and need. They want your message put simply so they can pass it along to others in a simple form. They don't have time for details, but they do have a great capacity to analyze you. Convey your passion for your data and what it means in the big picture. The C-suite is always thinking about the big picture, because it is their job to ensure the overall success of the company.

One of our female executive clients was reluctant to appear before the CEO, who she knew to be a notorious cross-examiner. Meetings with him were of legendary status with each successive executive recounting horror stories of "He did this and then he said that and . . ." Our client actually volunteered for this meeting. She suggested to the rest of the executive team, an all-male group, "Let me go first, and I'll find out just how bad it is."

She volunteered to go first for three reasons: First, she just wanted the meeting over with so that the anxiety of meeting with the CEO would no longer interfere with her day-to-day life. Second, she wanted to get a handle on the boss and learn how to "level the conversation" for future engagement with this important person. Third, she wanted to teach her male colleagues what personal initiative for the team was. "Frankly, I didn't trust any of them to represent us well enough. I wanted to go in and come out and teach them how to do it."

When summoned to the C-suite in any form, beware of three critical mistakes others have made: being so nervous that you ask not to present, deluging them with detail, or speaking off topic. Show up, think about their needs not yours, and stay on target. Also one more thing: Don't be offended when they interrupt you. They will, and it is a compliment! Answer their question directly, and never say, "I'll be getting to that a little later in my presentation!" Never, ever say that!

Be prepared, but don't assume too much. If they come up with something you're not prepared for, honor that and address it naturally and honestly. Never expect them to react in one way or another. They are leaders because they are charged with making decisions. Depending on their style, they have made decisions differently—some analytically, some emotionally, some from the gut, some with a few facts and lots of instinct, but they have made the tough decisions.

Even if you are high up in the echelons of your organization and are comfortable presenting to a large group of directors, you must enter every meeting with the mentality that no one cares more about this presentation than you do. Seating, volume, energy, and data will all work together either in your favor or against you in every opportunity you are given in which to exert your influence.

It is crucial to arrive at the room early and really examine the seating options. If you're in a hotel meeting room, ask the sales office to show you the room the night before. Form a picture of it in your mind's eye so that you can place you and your directors in that scenario. Hotel setup crews often follow a set schematic, and if you want that changed (for example from a U-shape to tables), then be very clear about your preference. Take caution if your group is larger than thirty in a U-shape. That arrangement can be awkward. Picture it: Ten people on each side of the U-shape, including the middle table. That's a lot of space in the middle, and you want to be able to maneuver within the U but not allow the participants to be so far apart that they can't hear well. Sometimes a classroom setup is preferred.

Now while this information is quite specific, the point we want to emphasize is that you need to be very aware of the environment of your meeting and that your part of the meeting is, in fact, your meeting. You are responsible for how it goes. Remember, if you don't take control of every situation that you can, someone else will . . . or won't!

Now it's up to you to provide the stellar opening act. Be highly energized, and inject as much personality as possible into your presentation. Now is not the time to be low-key! Give an example of your experience with the company to catch their attention; tie in some current event you read about in *USA Today.* Do anything to start on an energetic note so that the group looks forward to the rest of the meeting.

When you need to share the heavy data, do so with pride and enthusiasm. Take pauses to breathe, and allow the audience time to digest what they've heard so far. Walk back and forth away from the screen, and use your arm to point out something important. Walk back to the laptop, and address the group with vigor. Just because your audience is the upper echelon of the organization doesn't mean that they want to hear only straight facts. They want to hear some personality come through. This may be your time to shine!

Always follow up with the C-suite, but be sure to do so simply and with class. Why? Because they'll forget about you the moment you leave the room. They're on to other things, and a myriad other decisions that need to be made. We suggest a brief handwritten note—even if their assistant opens it first. It's personal and will at least capture their attention for a few moments. Send them follow-ups of value: updated articles you find that relate to the topic you presented, simple facts and data from news and research, and also small personal things that they may have confided in you about—like an article on a new bowling alley with a midnight bowl, say: "Know your son loves to bowl . . . thought you'd like to see this."

When you're the one in front of the top brass, remember, they've been around awhile. Strive to get to know them early in your career. Read about them, read their writings, books, and articles. Find out about their decision-making trends, and allow yourself to build a folder so when you're in front of them, you feel that you know them. They don't want a boring presentation. Of course they want documented data to make good decisions, but spice it up with colorful examples or vivid language in a form they can pass on. They don't want any extraneous humor or interactive activities. The worst sin here is to waste their time and attention. The all-important follow-up is something few people do. Follow up with a simple note, e-mail, or article.

When you are preparing to present to the top brass,

- Repeat the mantra, "Nobody cares more about this meeting than I do." Let that mantra take you through your presentation so that you are able to maintain your energy and passion.

- Take the stage with confidence. Your audience wants you to be successful. In smaller venues, move inside the U-shape; in larger venues, move out from behind the podium.

- Practice carefully the essence of your presentation. Essence is just what those who make big picture decisions are looking for. Once you can clearly state the essence, the rest of your detail is editable.

My advice to young women or new executives is to be consistent. I report directly to the CEO, and I don't change my talk fun-

damentally because the CEO is there. So be true to yourself;
stay on your game.

   Also "brand" yourself so that you are who you are; present
yourself authentically.

Michelle Gadsden-Williams
Vice President and Global Head,
Office of Diversity & Inclusion
Novartis Pharma AG

PART 4

Lead on Your Feet

25

The Sales Pitch

Even if you are not a salesperson—perhaps especially if you are not a salesperson—you will be selling, suggesting, showcasing, and influencing at each moment of each day.

You are continually presenting, and all the skills of the effective salesperson come into play. The good news is that when you are aware of the selling involved, you get a great deal more practice making your pitch—framing your message. The bad news is that you often don't have time to think about what worked and what you might do differently next time.

Know What Works for You

Know what works by being aware of what works for you. Throughout the day, reflect upon which of your ideas seemed to hit its target—whether in casual conversation, a full-blown presentation, or a contribution to a meeting. Be very conscious of how you come across to others, what makes sense to them, and how you are of value to them. When did your pitch hit home?

It's about the Receiver

In baseball, the pitch is the initiation of the game. While the pitcher does not want the batter to make contact with the ball, in our game, we certainly do want that contact—that connection—to happen. It will happen at your initiation. Don't be afraid to help someone else get in the game by initiating. Sales professionals and executives alike know that their initiation is critical to the conversation that will enable them to inform, persuade, negotiate, sell, and influence. Never take your eye off the other. Be aware of them, work with them, see their value, be of value to them, and always know they are the building blocks of your growing success.

When you consider what your pitch is, make sure you are looking at it from the receiver's point of view. This is known as relating the benefits to the buyer or user. When you simply describe your service or product, that is known as a feature. Features are fine and good, but we buy based on benefits—perceived benefits. Many in sales today still list features without suggesting benefits. "Our hotel bed is adjustable" is a feature. "Our hotel bed adjusts to each person on the bed, which allows you and your spouse a good night's sleep, just like at home, or better!" is a feature *and* a benefit.

While the foregoing may be obvious to experienced salespeople, just listen to most pitches that fill your days. Very few will be hooked to a benefit. If there is one thing in this book that will make you a star at any level, sharing the benefits of your ideas, products, or services is it.

Don't Communicate—Connect!

Connection supercedes communication. People who connect really make a difference in the lives of others as well as in their own lives. Relationship is a vital component of any human interaction. It is the basis of the ever-present handshake, smile, and opening greeting. Don't stop there. Allow your eyes to engage, your interest to pique, your words to paraphrase, and your contribution to any conversation to be connective and enriching.

Rehearse "What If"

All of this takes an engaged, active mind constantly in search of how to convey the *what* and the *why* to the *who* of their world when the time presents itself. Rather than memorization, employ quiet, inner rehearsals. Living with a what-if attitude will do that for you over time. When you are at a meeting, what if you are asked to speak? At a conference, what if your partner doesn't show up? In the car on the way to the sale, what if your boss quizzes you on the customer? Rehearse your pitch in your mind so that it connects naturally when you have to play ball.

Don't Pitch—Catch!

What we're saying is that your sales pitch is less a pitch and more of a catch—of the other's reactions to your comments and questions. When you try too hard—when you focus on features and product and self, you set yourself up for losing the sale. When you are instead open, with your catcher's mitt up—you stand a chance of catching the feedback of your idea buyer. As a woman, you're a great catcher. Catch the feedback of your listener, and toss the ball back to him or her with skill. Dale Carnegie is famous for teaching influence via listening. He coached salespeople to let the buyer define the product he or she wanted. And the only way to do that is to "catch" that definition by listening.

> *Women are naturally attractive to men. That gives them a great advantage [in selling ideas]. But you have to be yourself. Don't try to "be like a man" because you think that gives you more credibility.*
>
> Bill Kurtis
> Kurtis Productions

26

Showcase Your Services

The showcase, or short demonstration of services, is a classic method of presentation at large meetings, expos, and conferences. The healthcare industry calls it the poster session—a review of scientific data or clinical studies, while the consumer-products industry uses short trade booth presentations to display new trends. In the professional speaking industry, speakers present samples of their keynotes at bureau showcases in front of meeting planners. The showcase is also a requirement for some job interviews. Trainers and facilitators are often asked to present a sample training module from a longer program. Pharmaceutical representatives present product information in this format as well. Actors and actresses, even famous ones, have to come in and compete for the role by showing what they can do. Bottom line—if you are able to showcase well, it will be career boosting for you and financially rewarding for your organization.

From trade shows to job interviews to poster sessions, showcasing your services or products in a limited amount of time presents a challenge. You may be thinking, *What do I bring? What will grab the eye and the ear of the potential buyer? Can the buyer make the leap from what they know to what I am presenting?* When time is limited, it is a tough format to plan for. Yet, short events and presentations provide a great opportunity for valuable face-to-face time, and the response to interpersonal impressions is significant. These opportunities provide an open entrance to you, your skills, and your talents. You can accomplish a lot in fifteen minutes or less—even in five—but only when you prepare and proceed with a purpose.

Connect Immediately

Because showcases involve a number of presenters, you will typically be working with a meeting planner or internal contact whose job it is to inform you about the rules, timing, and expectations of the event. Typically, the planner or her assistant is present at the event and is your first point of connection. When you arrive, use your contact person's name immediately—as you introduce yourself. For example, "Hello, John, I'm Sharon Smith." This shows you did your homework. Immediately repeat the contact's name after he or she introduces herself or himself. This shows you are listening. "Thank you, John, for the opportunity to give you an overview this morning." Look the contact in the eye and shake hands firmly with a friendly smile. This communicates both etiquette and confidence.

Dress the part: be clean, crisp, well put together. Your appearance is very, very important, especially when you have a short amount of time to make an impression. Speak confidently right away—as soon as the clock starts running; the first few lines are very important to keep the person's attention. Communicate that you know exactly what your strengths are and why you're there. Notice what others say about you, how they compliment you, what their demeanor is with you. All of these are clues to how you are coming across. Impressions under the duress of a short time frame happen often not from our content, but from our context—how we look, act, respond, and engage.

Sound the part. In a showcase, every word you choose will be heard more intently. Watch how you refer to others or the audience. Your choice of language may give away your age, gender, or regional background. Avoid words such as *you guys, awesome, y' know, like,* and *y'all.* Instead simply say, *you* or *Our clients prefer,* or *Many of you . . .* or *exciting, record-breaking*—words that sound more professional than colloquial. Your vocabulary will set you apart from your peers, especially when those in the room are older or more senior in their positions. Every time you showcase, every time you present, every time you have an influential moment, you are "on," and they are evaluating. Make no mistake, personnel decisions happen here more than anywhere else.

Be Unique

Don't try to borrow other people's material, techniques, stories, or examples. Someone will have heard or seen them before. Kevin once took copious notes on one side of a napkin, made recommendations on the spot on the other side, and then gave the napkin to the client. Six months later, while speaking on the phone, the client said, "I am looking at that napkin you gave me from the 410 Club. I use it every day." That is influence on the fly and proves that you can think on your feet! You can also imagine how impressed Kevin was with his client. It works both ways. Kevin even says he prefers to use napkins because they are unique; they deliver the punch of immediacy, are in the moment, and completely personalized. Find ways to be "with" the other person, and you will be memorable because you will be one of a kind—uniquely you.

Tell Your Stories, but Edit Them

Good stories may result from client successes, failures that resulted in positive change, or relatable events of daily life, like shopping or being on a plane, that tie into your purpose. In a shorter format, keep them brief with an immediate learning point. Others may have your facts or the same market research. Nobody will have your stories. Be on the cutting edge. Your content dates you more easily than you would guess. Don't use old theories without a very good reason. Chances are someone has heard them. Your stories and testimonies are unique because they are yours. Stories illustrate and teach and, best of all, lead others.

Where do you find stories? You simply need to stay aware of what is coming your way, what experience you are stepping into, and who is there. Then when you have a good story, tell it to a few people naturally throughout your day, and check their reaction. As you learn to tell the story, you will notice the connective points of the story for them. This then becomes your refined story.

Be Specific and Timely

Busy people today want specific solutions to problems. Most likely, that's why they're attending your showcase session—to get specific ideas or impressions in a short amount of time. Involve the audience with simple questions, even in this format. This "interview" helps you attend to the specific needs of the audience right away. Credibility comes with an on-the-spot ability to apply information to experience. The way you reel in relevant information is through Q and A and genuine interest in the concerns of your audience.

We often work with industries that are not part of our formal training—pool building, medicine, produce marketing, nonprofits, and up to seventy-five other industries per year. We don't have to pretend to know the ins and outs of the business; we need only ask good questions, listen with interest, and apply what we learn to our key concepts. We said to a pool manufacturer once, "There is a lot more to this family business than digging holes in the ground." The response was immediate. The client said, "You do know this business, don't you? The diggin' part is easy, the family part—well, you know!" Credibility comes from your relationship, not only from your content.

How can you make the most of a showcase format? The audience is thinking, *How will this work for my customer? What will this person do in front of my clients if I give them this work? How will this person handle problems and on-the-spot service?* You can't blame them for wanting specific answers. Give them the best of you in a short time. One of the best ways to do that is to ask them questions right away, before you panic under the threat of time. Ask them for their greatest challenge, their burning questions, and their most recent tough customer. Then answer those issues, and you'll have their attention for the duration. There's a lot you can get done in a restricted time frame.

When you have a limited amount of time with your audience, consider

- Evaluating your level of personal interaction. How would you describe the way you come across to others in business? Look at all aspects of your interaction with others—manner, clothes, initiative, and language. This "inventory" can be a revealing process.

- Keeping a story list or beginning a journal. Your own experiences can be great teachers, sources of humor, and poignant moments for an audience. These notes will become your signature pieces, and you can craft and recraft them to convey the essence of your thinking. One way the professionals do it is to first use them in casual conversation with many different types of people, and watch their reactions. Comedians often use this approach to change a word here or some timing there before they use a joke onstage.

- Finding the essence of your content first. How would you get it across in three minutes or less? Keep the content easy to digest, and remember: If you can explain it in three minutes, then you can easily expand it to ten, fifteen, or twenty minutes.

Keep in mind that people's questions might consume a good amount of time. If you've got only thirty to forty-five minutes, don't let questions take you off track. Manage the participation of the audience; commit to taking questions offline if need be. Take control.

Amy Huntington
President
Juno Lighting Group

27

Train from 1 to 100

Employee development is taking on a greater emphasis; the American Society for Training and Development State of the Industry Report 2007 shows companies are spending more on training than ever before. The ability to train others to do good work is grounded in effective speaking and listening skills. Whether you train one person who directly reports to you or travel across the country training everyone in your company, you'll need to prepare for the learning environment, engage your audience, and verify the results you achieved through concerted listening and questioning.

Know What Training Is and What It Is Not

Training is not spewing forth facts and data for memorization and regurgitation. The trainer is not an all-knowing guru, but a skilled facilitator of adult learning. Training is helping people be effective and current in their jobs. An effective trainer presents new information so that it relates clearly with what the learner already knows. Adults tend to be "experience rich and theory poor" when they come to the corporate classroom. When you are training from one to one hundred employees, you have the responsibility to make learning relevant and meaningful.

Many adults in corporate work have a mixed reaction to training. Some have had such poor trainers and training courses that the very word makes them cringe. Others are so interested in developing themselves that they jump on the chance to spend time learning. You can cut through any negativity by being aware of this double-edged sword and helping yourself by seeing real training as education. The old saying, "Give me a fish, and I eat for a day—teach me to fish, and I eat for a lifetime," presumes you want fish in the first place! Always find out from those you are training how they feel about it, what they most want, how they want to learn it, and how they will use it. This level of engagement shows respect, and it makes your job easier. Don't shoot ideas at them in the dark; simply ask, and you will see the cooperation light up. It is the learner who can teach you.

Plan the Best Environment for Learning

One of the biggest mistakes trainers make is rushing the process. A hastily reserved room, lack of workbooks, or slow Internet connection can signal to the learner that this training is of low priority. In addition, rushing through the material does nothing to encourage but instead confuses. Every detail you plan for the person you're training is important. Be sure to allow time for opening small talk and questions—even one on one. If at all possible, conduct the training in an area that is comfortable and allows privacy. If you must train in a busy area of the office, let nearby employees know you would appreciate their cooperation on noise level and interruptions.

If you have a training room or large meeting room, set the chairs in a U-shape or circle to encourage discussion. If the group is more than thirty, sit classroom style or at tables, and build in movement and mingling throughout the day so all are energized. Have snacks and drinks available, or take a break at midpoint. Keep in mind that attention spans grow shorter every year due to technology and our fast-paced society. Any handouts or booklets should be ready to go and computers in working order so you can use your time wisely.

Present with Energy

Learners sense when you're being overly enthusiastic or bored with the material. Be yourself, but always with clear energy supporting the training and its benefits. Maintain an open stance; don't lean on tables or desks as you may have seen others do. Move around the room, and keep the lights up at all times. Use charts, handouts, small props, and computer visuals as well as video, DVD, and Internet visuals to vary your presentation. Be alert to speaking in a monotone; if you sense you are, change something—your position, their positions, your visuals, their handouts—anything to provoke attention.

Engage Your Learners

Adults learn best when they apply knowledge to their everyday work. Begin by asking questions such as, "What challenges you most about this new material?" or "What are you looking forward to learning today?" Never assume you know the mind-set of those you train. Their burning questions will help you know what to emphasize. Once you have an idea of their thoughts and fears, present the information accordingly. Use examples to make facts, rules, and regulations come alive. Industry-relevant examples encourage the learner to apply new material to his or her own world. Intersperse questions throughout your training, such as, "What questions do you have now?" or

"What can I make more clear at this point?" This prompt will encourage your learner to interact. Use these techniques with one to one hundred. In either case, learners typically have questions they're afraid to ask without encouragement. Pause after you ask a question. Don't answer it yourself. If you pause and count to five, someone will almost always respond.

Facilitate Their Wisdom

Busy people don't have time to ask themselves the right questions, let alone process the answers. When you are training a group, you play the role of facilitator—one who encourages discussion and makes it easy. If a group is reluctant to respond individually, try asking small teams of three, or partners, to share insights with each other first. Then ask them to share with the whole group. We have found that clear, thoughtful questions are the best way to stimulate adults to apply information. They are better than Tinkertoys, puzzles, endurance activities, and case studies. These other trainer games and techniques can be fun and helpful at times, but questions get at the real issues. Trust that and ask them. You will rarely be disappointed.

Questions are important, but carefully listening to the answers is more so. A good trainer knows asking is the easy part. The summarizing, listing, checking, and projecting the answers forward is the challenge. As a facilitator, you must first and always verify what you've heard before stating your own opinion or what the materials say is correct. As learners get accustomed to your ability to listen, they'll feel more and more comfortable getting involved with you and the material, and your results will be positive.

When you are the trainer,

- Don't rush the process. Plan your setup, your learning tools, and the questions you'll ask to warm up the group. This thoroughness will pay off in the long run, making the rest of the interaction easier.

- Ask questions, and then really listen. Don't jump in with your idea of the answer. Adapt your presentation accordingly.

- Give up details for broader concepts that adults can apply to their own work. They will respect your willingness to make learning relevant.

The Women's Leadership Program at my college had a woman make a presentation to the group on how to understand the results of our Myers-Briggs personality tests. She secretly seated the audience according to personality type and then asked everyone to complete a task with their neighbors, giving each group markers and paper. When she asked each group to display their work, it was obvious we had been organized by our type; while each person at my table thought similarly, the differences between the tables were clear and striking! She taught us about ourselves and how we could relate to other types of people by giving us direction instead of a lecture. I could think of no better way to facilitate discussion and understanding.

Elizabeth Wailes
The George Washington University

28

Capture the Keynote

The keynote is the most important speech at a conference because it carries the central theme. The keynote speaker or keynoter is the person who delivers that speech. The female keynote speaker is a rarity. Men tend to dominate the keynote arena, largely due to the fact that men continue to dominate the executive arena. When you, the female presenter, earn the keynote, you represent not only yourself and your organization, but also your gender. The women in the audience are in awe of you, and there is not one who wouldn't appreciate being asked to be standing right where you are. As a woman, know that this is an opportunity to present yourself in the strongest light possible. Own the stage. Don't just deliver information. Design an experience that no one else can give; customize beyond what is expected. Bring your unique perspective. That's why they asked you to keynote, and that's what the audience came to hear.

You've Earned It—Work It

Cyndi still remembers attending a luncheon keynote delivered seventeen years ago by a well-known female French executive of a pricey champagne company. The event was a place to see and be seen, the ticket price was hefty, and the event glistened; women chatted over champagne, and finally the beautifully coifed speaker took the stage, dressed in a very French little black dress and following a stellar introduction.

But that's where stellar ended. To Cyndi's and the rest of the audience's dismay, the talk was a loosely held-together set of disorganized stories ending twenty minutes early. She felt a loss, a disappointment, and anger. Others did, as well, and the postspeech commentary that day was bitter. Don't let your audience down. If you are honored with the keynote, work it—really work it! Do your customizing homework. Ask about the audience. Have the timing (traditionally thirty to fifty minutes) down pat; practice with a coach or your most trusted colleagues, and absolutely use your best stuff!

What is your best stuff? It is your experiences. It is the stories and lessons you've learned along the way. Whether you're talking about personal achievement, incredible financial success, or entrepreneurial risks you've taken, you're there to convey your essence. Each story is tied with a learning point. Make it a point that the audience can relate to. Find the common ground, and provide the substance to support it.

Lighten Up and Engage

A keynote does not have to be entirely substance. It also does not have to be a totally didactic treatise from the podium. You have the option to include audience participation. Incorporate unexpected light moments. As you consider your substance, consider how the audience can apply your wisdom to their lives.

Ask them to remember something—their first job or the moment they knew they were in the field that they were meant to be in. We find this works very well with highly skilled audiences. Ask doctors when they knew their practice area was truly their calling. Ask teachers the same.

Another way to engage with your audience is to present them with a simple true-or-false quiz. At a very large conference for women in foodservice, an international author asked the audience to take a quick self-survey and share the results with their nearest tablemate. The results were energizing. While the speaker could not process all the answers, obviously, the point was made—that everyone had a unique experience with leadership.

A Touch of Humor Brings a Touch of Class

Maria Pappas, the treasurer of Cook County, Illinois is known for her ability to spew facts extemporaneously, impressing her audiences with her knowledge of the tax system. Yet, she has said, "If you can't make people laugh two or three times while speaking, you might as well be in the funeral business." Audiences love humor; actually, in a keynote, they expect it. Even if you are in the funeral business, there is an opportunity for humor. In fact, speakers who address the funeral industry often comment that funeral directors have their own unique appreciation of humor.

Rarely does humor mean telling jokes. Humor is very personal, and if you use humor in a keynote, you absolutely must test it to see if it is appropriate and really funny. We have both had experiences where the same humor has sailed with one group and flopped with another.

To illustrate, Cyndi tells an anecdote about being pleasantly surprised when a minister at her church, usually so boring that even his prayers are monotonous, told a refreshing story of his experiences as a World War II soldier in Switzerland. When she recounted it to students at a Catholic university, they laughed. When she told the same story to a group of creative, hip, urban art students, they didn't laugh at all. They were waiting for more.

The ability to keynote with humor is the mark of a truly experienced speaker. Be careful not to fall back on stories about your children or your flight in to the meeting. Those are too easy. Be creative. Poke fun at your industry or the current news or how the news is affecting your industry. Don't be too political unless that's what they are expecting. Applaud the world of the audience and honor that world, whether it be one of grocery produce markets or medical research.

When you are the keynote speaker, remember:

- The keynote address pays back in many ways you may not have considered. If you connect with one key person in the audience who becomes your champion, you have turned that short presentation into an opportunity to develop a productive relationship. You may catch the eye of a journalist or a media personality. You may catch the eye of an administrative assistant who has an "in" with her boss. Use this exposure to your advantage.

- Credibility and charisma both play a part. Spouting facts will appeal to some, but most will contact you again because they feel a personal connection. They like you and feel comfortable with you. When presenting the keynote, be yourself—with savvy.

- Lighten the load. Allow your keynote audience to breathe and enjoy the experience. They can do so with note taking, standing, mingling, sharing with a seatmate, or laughing. Let them have fun. Let them experience.

The biggest thing, however, is preparation. It is not unusual, even with my years of experience, for me to literally practice twenty to twenty-five times before I give a talk. I know my slides, I know my timing, and I'm ready.

Deborah Lee, MD, PhD

Baxter Healthcare

29

Be the Best MC

Once you are in a position of influence, the time may come when you will have to act as master of ceremonies at a meeting, whether it be small and informal at the office or on a larger, formal scale. At work, your MC duties might simply be introducing the agenda topics and speakers at the weekly meeting. At a conference, there may be a more formal expectation—involving biography sketches of guest experts or humorous anecdotes that link the events of the day. Both scenarios have a lot in common.

Role Requirements

The best MCs are crisp, clever, and crystal clear. Fundamentally, the MC must energize the room. Consider that your audience is basically looking forward to the next "act"— the next event. They really don't care much about you other than you had better know what's going on in case they don't. Many busy professionals don't even download the meeting agenda until they arrive. The best masters of ceremonies realize that, but they don't spend any time apologizing for it or thanking people for their valuable time away from their busy schedules.

When you are an MC, the most important thing to remember is that the focus is not on you. It is always something else—the next speaker, the next performance, the next activity, or the next meal. Keep that mind-set at all times, and it will carry you through those moments when you may feel unprepared or unfocused. You are, in essence, a cheerleader, helping the audience to keep their energy and to anticipate what's to come.

The MC must absolutely know the basic information that will relate those she is introducing to the reason they are there. We suggest three parts: something that builds credibility, something that adds fun, and something that ties the person to the rest of the day. For example:

"I am pleased to introduce our next speaker, Sharon Wright. Sharon brings fifteen years of sales excellence—primarily with key accounts—to our meeting today. When she is not selling, she is skiing—water skiing, that is—in any lake or ocean she can find. Sharon will speak on Capturing Key Account Strategies and provide a vital link to our goal of 20 percent increased profits."

You're Not Alone—Even When You're In Charge

The best MCs engage and encourage the audience to help them. They ask surefire questions: "How many of you have lost weight only to gain it back?" or "Raise your hand if you've ever replaced a teenager's lost cell phone." They challenge: "If you would like to hear from someone who could double your sales, yell, 'Yes.'" Or "If you're not having a good time so far, I dare you to stand up!" If the meeting is a small, more casual office gathering, you can still use questions to involve—just make them specific yet still upbeat. For example, "How many of you have noticed that Sally worked later than most of us this week?" or "How many of you are looking forward to hearing from our winning sales team? [Start applause.]"

Rarely have we seen this group style of questioning fail. That's because most adults like to immediately relate to information personally. Their tendency is to play along with anticipation of what might be ahead. You can use this technique in nearly any speaking venue. When you are sister of the bride, ask, "How many of you have traveled over three hundred miles to be here today?" When you are MC-ing the company retreat, ask, "How many of you went to camp as a child?" Hand-raising and nonthreatening questions are an easy way to bring the audience to the podium with you—metaphorically speaking. They share your spotlight for a moment.

Find the Common Ground

Some examples of common ground openers that unite the audience might be

* "Most of us here today would love to have more time to talk with each of our employees."

* "Those of us in the room today are here because we know, love, and respect Harold Cummings."

* "We are here tonight to honor someone we will miss deeply—Professor Williams."

* "We're here because we care . . . about our kids."

They're not that difficult to write if you simply consider the audience. What are the three key things the audience has in common? How can you allude to at least one of those in an embracing, nonthreatening manner?

Common ground is especially important when the audience is divided for some reason. Imagine a community group that is split on an issue or an executive board experiencing conflict. In those situations, it is especially important to cheerlead—but in an easy-to-digest manner that reminds people of what they have in common. The community group has passion for the neighborhood. The board wants to be financially solvent.

Vocal Considerations for the Female MC

The female voice is not so naturally geared to getting a crowd's attention as is the male voice—which has a deeper timbre and tone. When you are MC, use a mike when it's available. Request a microphone if the group numbers more than fifty. If a mike is not available, get the group's attention by asking them to tinkle a spoon against a glass with you or to clap hands with you. For example, "If you can hear me, clap once." "If you can hear me, clap twice." Do not start until you have their attention.

You can master the master of ceremonies role. Remember:

- You're the cheerleader. The MC is the hallmark of the day; you are there to build energy and participation in the room. The audience is looking to you to set the tone for a winning day.

- You're the clarifier. The MC is the one who knows what's next and why. Even though they have the program agenda in front of them, the audience is looking to you for the right information.

- You're the bridge. You help the audience move from one place to another, and you must act as a sturdy connector from point to point.

The toughest role I have is when I am asked to be the master of ceremonies for another organization's awards event—because I'm representing the organization, not myself. I have learned to have someone help me write my speech. A speechwriter makes what I say a lot better sounding. If you're asked to MC, don't take it lightly. It's important to have something you want to say—if you don't have anything to say, yikes!

Diane Kubal
President
Fulcrum Network

30

Present Bad News

Bad news need not always be presented in a bad way. Companies both large and small are accustomed to bad news. Approvals that were not passed, test results that disappointed, unexpected stock fluctuations, key personnel who are moving on—all have become routine in every field. Bad news, however expected, is still bad news. How you present the news will be seen either as spin or as a call to action. Spin—while essential to the culture of some highly competitive, cutting-edge industries—is seen by most as manipulation. The female presenter should be aware that this is not the time to be "nicey-nice" but instead to be "really real."

Wise presenters of bad news don't put on rose-colored glasses (a fake cheery demeanor); rather they share their disappointment, put it in context, and add a piece that says how we are all going to move on from here. Babe Ruth was well known for more strikeouts than home runs, yet his legacy is the home run. Edison failed more than he succeeded, but when he succeeded, he lit up our world. How have your staff risked, worked, contributed, and where are they in the context of the total effort? Capture that, and the bad news will not be so discouraging but rather will be seen as a bump in the road.

Keep It in Perspective

When presenting bad news, demonstrate empathy with your listeners to engage them, and then use your empathy to show them the new way, the new path, or the bigger picture. Whether or not empathy comes naturally to you, work to make this connection even if it seems a bit artificial at first. It is the key to your success in connecting with the audience. Nothing is worse than an unfeeling lecture by a cold leader devoted only to the bottom line.

Empathizing also works well when you have made a mistake. Admit it, and put it in context. Your staff knows you made the mistake, they know you are responsible, and they will support you when you affirm the truth. Let them know your thinking at the time. There are few better ways to build loyalty among a team than admitting the mistake everyone already knows you made!

Link It with the Context

Context comprises all the events that form the environment in which, in this case, the bad news takes place. When you understand context, you will come across as less judgmental or superficial. Context tells us about history and tradition as well as about the changes that have been brought about by special effort. Context means you are careful to remember the people, the places, and the things that make this place or time or people special. The founders, the philosophy, the vision, the first dollar are all contextual clues that will anchor your audience with you, especially when bad news is on the way.

The content of what you say needs to be carefully crafted but not scripted. Consider being straightforward and strong, sympathetic and direct, and understanding of the present with a focus on the future. You will have to straddle the line between "This is terrible" and "There is a new day dawning." The best way to do that is to link the bad news with the context and then transition to the actions to be taken. In this way, you will be constructing a new story— the story that will be remembered long after the facts are forgotten.

Connection is significant. How you look, how you speak, how you greet others, how you respond to questions and comments and criticisms will impact your message. Be very gracious, listen to the concerns of your audience, and take action to make positive change and turn over a new leaf.

There's good news about bad news:

- Your role is complex and requires you to prepare, but not script.

- Expectations will be high for your presentation, but what will be most remembered is how you affect the listeners with empathy and rapport.

- You can work closely with context, content, and connection in order to communicate effectively in difficult times.

For bad news, be totally honest, like a conversation with a family would be . . . this is hurting me as it hurts you. Use compassion, engage personally, and let them respond. Show that this is affecting you as well. If there is some good with the bad, say that too—this need not be the end of the world.

Tim McNamara, PharmD
Vice President, Clinical Research and
Medical Affairs
ISTA Pharmaceuticals
Irvine, CA

31

Honor and Award with Aplomb

"And now a few words from . . ." At some point in your career, you are going to be called on to "say a few words" about another person at a company event. For those spontaneous speaking opportunities, both formal and informal, your first priority is to make the other person look great. A little-known second opportunity is to look very good yourself. That is what the audience wants. Your appeal contributes to their experience.

Always Assume You Will Be Asked

Every time you attend a function, be prepared to be up in front of a microphone at a moment's notice. How should you do that? Think about the event—what do you know in advance about the key players and the program? Keep your eyes and ears open. When the honoree is being spoken about at your table, listen carefully.

If you have time to plan ahead, be sure you do so! The person who asked you to honor or award the other is expecting your best. Make some notes on a small card, and tuck them in your pocket.

Look and Sound As If You're Prepared

Take the stage. No matter how ill prepared you feel, fake it! Perhaps another way is to act as if you are prepared. Act "as if," and you will look "as if." Look out before you look down at any notes. Smile and scope out the audience. Then look at the person you're honoring. Only then, begin. Those critical few silent moments pack a punch because they are the mark of professionals.

Don't overtalk. Say just enough. Remember, this speech is not about you; it is about the other person. Keep it simple, and avoid *umm*s or *"and . . . umms"*—they are quite noticeable in a short introduction. Try beginning with three things about the person—for example, "When I think of Joe, I am remembering three things throughout his career," or "Susan has brought a wealth of skill and ability to us; in fact, there are three areas in which she shines." Other opening techniques include conveying an experience you had with that person, a metaphor, a funny quote, or even an adjective that best summarizes him or her. That is your anchor for the rest of all you will say.

Use humor. People expect this type of talk to be funny at some point. Everyone has something funny to relate to—a hobby or sport they're crazy about, their work habits, what they love to eat, or the music they like. Another idea is to pick something that is a bit extreme about them and emphasize that. Let your imagination go.

Have Something in Your Back Pocket

Everyone has one short lesson in life that they have learned—something a parent taught them, a philosophy learned from a pet, or a childhood experience. Keep that great one-liner in the back of your mind at all times to pull out and adapt. For example, "My Labrador retriever teaches me that life is about three things only, and these same three things are all about Joan, too. What three things? Food, fun, and safety. I think when you hear what Joan has done to earn this award today, you'll see that she is concerned about our nourishment, our camaraderie, and our comfort." The point is to have a "something" that always works.

So that you can always be ready to award and honor with class,

- Don't waste time apologizing or mumbling about not being prepared. It's about the other person, always.

- Immediately get to the heart of the matter—why the other person deserves the honor. Then blend in humor, funny incidents, and other data.

- Connect with the audience with your eyes. Keep notes on a small card so that you don't read them word for word. Glance up frequently.

One thing I wish I'd known when I began—you have to be sensitive to the person who hires you or asks you to speak as well as to the audience. The person who hires you is not necessarily tuned in to the audience. The president may hire you or interview you on the phone, but both customers [the president and the audience] must be kept in mind.

Karen Deis
President
Mortgage Speakers Bureau

32

Plan and Organize
with Authority

Many of you are or will be in charge of planning and organizing workplace meetings and events. You will be the person who updates the staff on meeting progress or who speaks at promotional events prior to the meeting. If you consider five key criteria, you'll be able to achieve the same great results that professional meeting planners do. And your experience will grant you important points of influence as a speaker in front of key decision makers.

First, Understand *Why*

While company meetings appear to be informational, what's really happening is much more complex. Ideas are being sold. Relationships are being solidified. Conflicts are being aired. Objections are being tested. What is the "real" goal of your meeting? Is it a new product overview, a platform to allow comfortable networking, or a marketing effort to progress the image of your department or company with potential buyers?

One thing is essential—while only a few attendees will remember the information, they will all surely remember the experience of the event. How they are invited, greeted, seated, and fed is a key element if you wish to succeed in sharing your information. Therefore, knowing why you want these attendees to come is important. The why is first—before the how, when, what, and where.

Fit the Environment to the Audience

Audience size, makeup, and mind-set are all important. Groups of fifteen or fewer can be comfortable at a large board table, but when in a U-shape, they will see each other better, and you will have more presentation flexibility. Your speakers will have more intimacy with the audience as well. While large leather chairs may be impressive, it is important to allow movement around the table to have small discussions and allow ease of access to food and drink. Too small a room will quickly affect morale, as will too large a room. Maximize the energy by getting rid of extra chairs and using only one end of the room. Take a tip from comedy clubs: You will want your audience close to your presenters. That allows for more interactivity and warmth.

A group over fifteen has different considerations. A U-shape can still work, but be careful that it doesn't get so large that people around the U can't hear each other. Some groups use round tables but use only five or six seats instead of the traditional eight to ten. That way all can face the front and have space to write and discuss. Room setup is your job. You care the most. Think through what you want to have happen. Some audiences need to talk and discuss, some need to sit and listen, and still others will need room for small subgroups. By the way, having a large room and breaking the attendees into smaller discussion groups is a highly effective way to keep energy in the audience. Resist the temptation to break up and move to other smaller rooms. Your overall event becomes harder to control, and the discussions can get untimely or off track without an overseeing facilitator.

Help the Presenters Look and Sound Great

Consider their experience level and the amount of access you will have to them before the meeting. Will there be an opportunity to practice? If so, you need to set this up ahead of time and account for time in the room.

It is very important for all presenters to know the room, and it is even more essential for those with key information and little experience in presentation skills to familiarize themselves with the space. You can troubleshoot any problems that might occur the next day.

Acoustics are important, especially for larger groups. Check that you have up-to-date sound equipment, microphones, and dividers for larger rooms. You never know when unexpected construction noises or fun in the next room can cause a distraction. Wireless lavaliere microphones set up and run by an expert audiovisual company are an investment that will guarantee and pay big returns. Don't skimp on what your audience can see and hear. Allow presenters to practice with the sound equipment.

Make the Budget Your Partner

Most meeting organizers want a bigger budget than they're given, and they learn to do a lot with a little. For example, you don't have to order a lot of costly desserts and breads as snacks and meals. Audiences today appreciate fruits, trail mixes, and mineral waters. Alcohol is another option—up to you to negotiate or offer, as a beer or wine option only.

You can save on paper handouts by listing important links and Web sites on one classy paper page. Product packaging and samples can be visual aids instead of expensive four-color handouts. If you have a large budget, you can be classy without being opulent. Again, keep food healthy rather than decadent, and keep visuals essential and simple rather than overblown and hefty; audiences appreciate simplicity most of the time because streamlined ideas are easier to understand.

Consider the Time Frame

Mornings are better than afternoons or evenings for attentiveness of the audience. Keep the breaks carefully timed. A ten- to fifteen-minute stretch is much easier to control than a half hour. If you're off-site, make sure the hotel understands the break times and how to manage refills and snacks. A noisy coffee refill has been known to destroy the concentration of the group at crucial content points.

The key consideration for time is that you must respect the audience's expectation that things will start and end on time, that you will control the overtalkers, and that you respect the busy schedules the audience has come from.

When you are representing your project team, do a quick survey of the team via e-mail on any important point. Administrative assistants and project coordinators are always valuable sources of general information about people they work for and with. One meeting planner made this call and found out that the CEO coming to the meeting was a fan of Diet Mountain Dew. Arranging for that beverage to be available ensured a very big smile from the special guest.

Ask questions of those who planned the previous meeting: What did they learn? Inquire about the previous month's sales presentation. Take advantage of the experienced person's expertise and use it. He or she probably learned something that can help you. The more you know, the better you'll be able to make an impact. When all is said and done, it will be your involvement from start to finish that will make your meeting a success.

To organize a smoothly run meeting,

- Be aware that you are creating an experience for your audience, not simply an event or a meeting.

- Know that the overall impact of this experience will be significantly judged by the quality of the room, the food, and the creature comforts as well as by the content.

- How you personally interact as a host and presenter yourself will dramatically affect the experience and attitude of the audience before, during, and after the meeting.

For all speakers, male or female, the initial challenge is connecting—quickly—with everyone in their audience. But it can be hard for speakers to establish instant rapport, especially in this age where we are accustomed to speed and stimuli . . . TV and movies come at us at breakneck speed, and even in business, electronic communications ensure we get almost instant gratification.

Jane Jackson Esparza
Cofounder and President
Cornerstone Speakers, LLC

PART 5

Create a Lasting Connection

33

E-mails, Memos, Letters, and More

Every time you open an e-mail, you are likely to ask yourself two split-second questions: What is this, and what does it have to do with me? Everyone else does this also. That is why you will have special kind of influential power when you answer those questions in the subject line or at least the first two short sentences of all your e-mails. You have influence and therefore power when your communications are clear and easy to respond to. If you leave them guessing, they may guess wrong and hit the DELETE key, or worse, they'll forward it to someone else because they are confused or simply annoyed. Take a quick look at your in-box. How many of those e-mails stand out and tell you precisely what you are to do with them, what is expected of you? Are those not the ones you'll be answering first? Yours can be in that group also if you answer the receiver's question, "What is this, and what does it have to do with me?"

Be careful with your e-mails. They can be your most effective way to communicate when they are executed properly. They are a great way to present yourself and your ideas. Don't rush through your e-mails. Treat them as what they are—an excellent opportunity to move your agenda forward and express yourself exactly as you wish. E-mails, for all their limitations, are really one of the ways we can have control over our message and our presentation of ourselves. One caution: Use the drafts folder liberally so that you can write and then edit later. Editing is the key to effective e-mailing. Keep your e-mails short and concise, and free from attitude, assumptions, or emotion that might interfere with your effectiveness.

For many in business today, e-mail, voice mail, and even old-fashioned paper letters are not what we think they are. We think they express our message. In fact, they really are intended to elicit cooperation from the person receiving the message. Whom do you think about when you write—yourself or the receiver? You should be thinking first and foremost about the receiver of the message and what you want him or her to know and do with your message.

Take Time to Frame

You can have an additional edge in business with men by taking the time to frame your e-mail message carefully. So, consider what you want to say to him. What has he done well lately? What is the context for this message? What encouragement can you give him that is specific and real? This is not a time for empty compliments. This is a time to let him know that what he said at the last conference call had meaning, that what he contributed to the team meeting was well received, and that his last e-mail to you helped you to come up with a new idea.

We all skim e-mails. Write your e-mail accordingly: short, bulleted, focused, concise, and with a call to response and action. Attach your wordy documents, data, PowerPoint files if you need to, and label them for action as well. Remember, readers skim. Heavy text in an e-mail shouts "Read this later" to your recipient.

Reflect first, don't write. Consider, *What is this, and why should they attend to it? Who are they, and what do they know about this topic? What do I want them to know and do as a result of this e-mail?* Then write. Then put it in your draft folder, and at another time do a quick review with the respondent in mind. Try this for just a week, and notice what happens to you and to your responses from them.

Female executives we have interviewed have shared with us that managing females is more difficult than managing males, and that you have to be careful in how you craft your e-mails. Why? Competition, suspicion, questioning, talking behind your back, comparisons, and a host of other poisons are alive and kicking in the workplace. Try a new antidote: Just be nice! When we are nice, encouraging, and helpful to other women, we elicit the best from others.

The Extra Mile Need Not Be a Long One

E-mails that compliment, encourage, and go the extra mile are responded to in kind. Don't send e-mails when you are angry, and don't let someone else's snarky e-mail mess up your day. Remember, when emotion is involved, use the drafts folder. E-mail is no place to work out conflict.

E-mails that encourage and notice improvement also subconsciously train our staff and our colleagues (even our bosses) to be optimistic and keep working hard. Use your day-to-day e-mail to train and retain your key staff by making sure there is something coming through your e-mail that is gracious, honoring, and friendly. Be genuine here. Everything about your e-mail must be authentically *you*. And *you* must remain consistent with your tone, your intention, and your follow-through. The best thing others can say about you is that your e-mails are consistent with the way you present yourself in the office and in meetings. This kind of consistency is admired and valued, and it gets your message heard.

The undeniable truth for the female executive is that you are on display 24-7, and you need to carefully manage each step of your career, even down to your e-mails. When you are "on" that much of the time, be consistent in how the outer you represents your inner challenges, conflicts, and workplace competition.

When your correspondence is sent to those outside of your own team, make sure that you are complete in your wording, avoiding abbreviations and the alphabet soup of project names and roles that only your team would know. Spell it out so there is absolutely no confusion. One PhD remarked to us that he worked on a project for six months that was coded with letters he didn't understand. Finally, he found out what the letters meant. "I was too embarrassed to ask," he said with a smile.

Correspondence that goes to customers and those outside your organization need to be especially jargon-free and easy to understand. Keep them short and to the point with clearly friendly greetings and appreciative closings. Some closings we've seen, like "Cheers" or "Best," can sound too abrupt when you're outside the culture that uses them frequently. Also, the phrase "Hope this helps" is used so often that it appears less than sincere.

When you are crafting e-mail, remember:

- Present yourself as a consistent, valuable, approachable, and nice person at all times—but especially in an e-mail.

- Use encouragement liberally.

- Understand the concise language of the men, and respond to them appropriately. Be appreciative and approachable with women. You will be less of a target for resentment.

Use words of confidence. Men say things like "attack the competition, own the marketplace." Women say, "I think we should . . ." versus "We should . . ." In a woman's attempt to build consensus, she comes across as weak simply in the way she uses words versus how men speak.

Shawn Tomasello
Vice President of Sales and Training
Celgene Corporation

34

Preinterview to Ensure Success

Never give a presentation again without preinterviewing the audience. This can be a select group if you wish, or three or four, or twelve or twenty. Always interview. When you do so, you can immediately count on having that many advocates in the audience. For women, asking questions and listening is fairly easy and natural; it is part of your conversational style. Yet many do not take advantage of that ability to gain audience buy-in.

This phenomenon applies to any industry and any audience. Moviemakers "preview" movies to selected groups to gauge interest. Focus groups help advertisers see which particular commercial has appeal. You can do the same. Want to know what your audience is hungry for? Just ask.

The preinterview is the interview you conduct over the phone for ten minutes getting a sample of the audience concerns, their role in the company, their greatest challenges. Interviews help us gain information about an article we might be writing or some in-depth information needed. A preinterview is purposely devoted to only one thing—your presentation. As such, it is short, focused, and solely intended to help you get background information.

The best way to connect with your interviewee during the preinterview is to play what one of Kevin's professors called the "dumb nut." Act like a nonexpert, and ask a lot of questions, even if it is your field of expertise. The advantage of being a nonexpert is that it helps relax the person being interviewed.

Consider for a moment a presenter interviewing you. Usually the presenter is seen as an expert, a superior, or a star. And here they are, asking you for your expertise. The psychological shift is significant. Kevin once met Chicago's Mayor Daley on a flight from D.C. to Chicago. The mayor was behind him in the check-in line without guards or an entourage. "Well, hello, Mr. Mayor," he said. The mayor then went on to inquire about Kevin. "Tell me about yourself, Kevin," he said. On went the conversation with the "important" person asking the questions and showing the interest. Be inquisitive, and you'll learn more.

Try some standard questions that always engage the interviewee:

- "What, lately, has been your greatest challenge with regard to—?"

- "I'm confused, can you tell me a little more about that?"

- "What would you suggest the others in attendance do about that?"

- "How is that working for you?"

- "Is that seen as a big problem where you work?"

- "How big a problem is that for them? For you? For the profession?"

- "What kind of decision-making process do you use personally when you are evaluating—?"

- "If you were giving this presentation, what would your essential message be?"

- "I don't understand, can you give me an example of that?"

Our very favorite question, however, is the "most challenging part of your job" question because you can ask it of almost any person at almost any time for almost any reason! Everyone knows the answer to the question, "What do you find lately is the most challenging part of being a—?" What happens is that the person searches one of two places within: the pride spot or the pain spot. Either way, you are about to find out a significant clue to this person. It benefits you, the interviewer, because these concerns are usually the top-of-mind concerns. It benefits the interviewee because no one before has asked that question, and answering it is clarifying for them.

When conducting a preinterview, make sure that your entire focus is on the other person. What they disclose with these questions is important to them. The speaker gets an opportunity to really know the inner workings of the company this way. When we consult for a team, we always preinterview, and in doing so we learn a great deal about the team and the company, and the team "thinks" that we know a lot as well. That perception helps us work better from day one.

As you prepare to interview, remember:

- No matter how good your presentation is, any presenter can benefit from another advocate in the audience. Use the input gathered from your preinterview to connect with your audience during the presentation. Lyndon Johnson used to say that as a politician, every handshake was worth 250 votes. In your case, every interview means at least one more advocate, one more fan, and one more supporter of your message.

- Listen carefully to language used by your interviewee. How do they express the issue or the problem? What are their sources? What do they seem to feel they "know" that you'd like to correct or realign?

- End your interview with a recap of what you heard them say. Summarize it in their terms. You might quote exact words to give them an intimate experience of being understood. After an interview, it is common for the interviewee to wonder if he or she was heard, or if their words will be taken out of context. A final recap will help them and you.

Great female presenters handle themselves with confidence, knowledge, and believe in what they are talking about . . . they have content integrity. How you deliver is as important as your content. If you are weak on your delivery, they won't hear your message or you. Poorly prepared presenters focus so much on what to say that they don't listen to the audience. Know your audience. Gauge the audience; their look, their body language, and their questions. You may have to adjust.

Jeri Stewart, MS, RN
National Director
Clinical Science Managers
Abbott Immunology

35

Don't Break at the Coffee Break

If conversation is easy for you, you are one of the lucky ones who probably enjoy the coffee break. You'll take the opportunity in the coffee line to ask for feedback or ideas or just to get to know the person next to you. However, if you're more of an introvert, the coffee break is nothing more than downtime to be alone. You zoom to the coffee line, grab a cup quickly, and go check your phone messages. That can be a missed opportunity not only to connect with colleagues, but also to enhance your influence and your career as well. While there is nothing wrong with being an introvert, if you tend to be one, make sure you manage your career and your appearance to others carefully. While extroverts may seem to get all the attention, those who provide value and are visible in the process really get ahead. There is no room for false modesty in the workplace today.

Influence Casually

Most of us have heard about real business happening on the golf course. That's true of the coffee break as well, but not so obviously. It's the time for casual chat and making connections. Using that time well takes initiative. It's fairly easy to ask anyone about the situation or the event. Questions like,

"I noticed you nodding when I mentioned the IT team. What has your experience been?" or "Your last name is Anderson [looking at name tag]. What nationality is that?" or "Have you been to this conference before?"

The Extra Edge

That is why frequent or professional presenters go to the dinners, the cocktail parties, and the exhibit areas. That is why they mingle with the audience just prior to their presentations—it gives them an edge that helps them connect. Whether you are an introvert or an extrovert, your presentations must reflect your understanding of the people in front of you and their sometimes hidden feelings, agendas, and visions. What a powerful presenter really wants to hear is the quiet voice inside the participants that says, *She really knows. This is good stuff for me.* It is that simple. And it is that complex.

Every Place Breeds Connections

Conferences are great places to learn, to network, and to position yourself and your company for success. Even though many of the people there may be your competitors, treat them as collaborators in the learning process. Again, be a good listener, and their doors will open up to you. Avoid any competitive conversation about whose product is superior. Just go into active listening mode. The material you learn by listening can be very valuable to your boss and to you.

When you are attending a conference, it is common to bring and to share business cards with others in the hope of establishing connections with them, perhaps doing business with them in the future. But don't be too quick doling out your card. In fact, consider not having any with you at all. Instead, get their cards! That way you can follow up at your discretion. Simply say you don't have any cards but that if they give you their card, you'll follow up with your contact information.

When you give them your card, it is likely to be tossed within twenty-four hours. If you keep their card and then follow up with a note of thanks or an article of mutual interest, you are positioned as more valuable. When you get another's card, write a note on the back of it right away in their presence so that they know you are serious about following up.

Steady the Pace

The longer the social time frame, the more you must pace yourself. Don't start too strong or you'll be left without a direction. Don't talk about yourself first. Ask questions first. Be easygoing. Be memorable. Be complimentary. Be real. The goal is to learn about them, not about you. Focus on the goal.

To engage your social skills,

- Know that relationships can develop in any situation and be ready to inquire, to listen, and to encourage. Doing so makes you special and memorable.

- Focus on the other person. When you do that, you avoid the number one mistake many people make: They talk incessantly about themselves. No one wants to hear about you; they want you to hear about them. Know and practice this little used secret, and watch what comes your way.

- Begin by building trust. Trust is the key component of any relationship. Be a confidante, do what you say you will do, be encouraging.

You should still look female. Let your work determine how you are to be judged for what you bring to the table, male or female. At business dinners, don't let your guard down. You really never do get a second chance here. Those who drink too much at dinner create impressions that last for years and are difficult to turn around. Always ask yourself how you want to be perceived. A one-time lapse in judgment is remembered.

Seek feedback. Feedback should not be seen as negative. Ask other women, your seniors, how you look, how you did. Listen to them.

Jeri Stewart, MS, RN
National Director
Clinical Science Managers
Abbott Immunology

36

Effective Phone Communication

Have you noticed that business telephone communication has taken on a new level of importance? While at work, we tend to use e-mail or instant messaging for information transfer, everyday instructions, confirmations, and check-ins, often saving the phone call for more important matters. In fact, we schedule phone appointments on our calendars and commit to important telephone conferences regularly. Effective phone communication has become more valuable to your success than ever, and certainly a point of influence for you—the female professional.

Practice the Three C's

There are three things to keep in mind when you are on the phone: clarity, conciseness, and connection.

- **Clarity**—you have less opportunity for very clear communication because you are working with vocal communication only; you've lost the visual aspect of the message. Being with the other person live, seeing their nonverbal signals, and responding to them with your own is not possible, and therefore, what you say and what you hear are of highest importance.

- **Conciseness**—keeping things simple and speaking to the essence of your message are of primary importance if you are to clearly communicate on the phone. This is not the place to ramble on, but unfortunately many people do, and phone conversations take much longer than they should.

- **Connection**—this is the whole point of the conversation, or it should be. Connection is not only for the one-on-one interpersonal aspect of our communication; it is also to assure that the message is taken seriously and acted upon.

Many of us think we are clear, concise communicators. Recall, however, your last phone call. How did you perceive the other person? Was he or she lacking in any of the three C's noted above? Were you?

Use Notes as Your Ally

The great thing about planned telephone calls is that you have time to do your homework. You can search the Internet for information about the other person as well as make notes you can use freely, since the other won't know you have them front of you! While preparing for phone calls may be a revolutionary move on your part, it is always worth the effort. The caller may throw you off guard or surprise you. Your planning and notes will get you through.

Also, take notes as you talk and listen so that you are focused and not distracted, so that you respond instead of react, and so that you have a record of what was said.

Listen with Vocal Responses

Paraphrase frequently, using the terminology employed by the other. These are called "notes quotes," a highly powerful influential technique. Every person at the other end of every phone call has one thing in mind: "Do you understand what I am telling you?" Add your ideas gradually and only after you have listened well. To be able to paraphrase well any-time, but especially on a phone call, is the mark of a skilled communicator. Paraphrasing is also time-saving because you'll get the message correctly the first time—rather than after several follow-up questions and quizzical e-mails.

Partner with the Other on the Call

Consider connecting even better with phrases such as "I need your help," "Can you give me some detail on," "Can I run something past you for your input," "I'm working on a draft of the report." In this way, you begin to get the other's input and buy-in, which will help build agreement later.

Partnering does not mean losing your assertiveness. Women, especially, can sound subservient on the phone. Keep your voice firm and calm, and work as an equal part-ner solving a problem and collaborating.

Ask for and Give Summaries

Summarize when you are nearing the end of the conversa-tion. Just ask to recap or to summarize not only the action item but also their assessment and their feelings as ex-pressed in the phone call. This attention reinforces for them that they were heard. If you disagree, make sure that you are respectful of their opinion while you are presenting yours. Saying, "I have a slightly different perspective," will help you get your idea across without them becoming overly de-fensive.

Don't End at the End

Follow up in some concrete form. Have a tangible way for the other person on the line to remember the conversation. This could take the form of a short e-mail immediately afterward, an article sent with a Post-it Note on it, a hand-written thank-you, or some concrete next step for action (even a draft of an e-mail you will be sending to someone else). When you follow up, the other person feels the momentum and is more likely to be engaged as well.

Receive Calls with Grace

When you're on the receiving end of a call, answer in a friendly manner, no matter your mood at the moment. Your telephone greeting should always—not sometimes, but always—sound upbeat and professional. (So should your voice mail greeting.) Identify yourself and your department; or at the least, identify yourself with every answer.

While you may talk in a chatty style to your friends, your phone voice at work should be consummately professional. This means using "hello" instead of "hi" as a greeting. It means saying, "How are you?" not "How ya doin'?" or "What's up?" Your tone should be as naturally low-pitched as you can, without a squeaky sound. Practice your greeting, and use the same one over and over so callers know what to expect.

If you're not able to talk long, ask for an alternative time, again in a kind manner. Offer to be the one to call back. You can also alert the caller to the amount of time you have: "Joe, I would love to hear about the meeting; I have about five minutes now, or I would be glad to call you back."

For effective business phone calls, follow these guidelines:

- Prepare for every call with the business purpose in mind.

- Make sure the other person on the call is clear about what the call is about.

- After your normal greeting, take charge of the call if you initiated it. The other person frequently wants to know, "What is this about, and what does it have to do with me?" After opening pleasantries, get right to the issue and its impact or relevance to the listener.

- Be aware of the distraction factor.

- Understand who you are representing.

- Speak as if you were being recorded.

- Use the speakerphone with care and discretion.

You can apply all the guidelines above to teleconferences and Web seminars, too. However, teleconferences and "Webinars" require some additional considerations due to the group environment. To make a great impression on teleconferences and Webinars, consider these tips:

- Prepare for these activities even more than you would for an in-person meeting.

- Have your notes laid out on your desk.

- Use names frequently—yours and others.

- On Webinars, refer regularly to what others are seeing on their computer screen.

- Beware of the temptation to distract yourself.

- Know that you cannot multitask without loss.

- Be careful of e-mailing during the Webinar, especially if you are being critical of the leader or a member of the group.

E-mail communication completes the picture of your telecommunication skills at work. Deceptively quick and simple, e-mail has bred many bad habits and undermined many a career. Never take e-mail for granted. Use it with the utmost professionalism. We suggest you follow the rule of imagining that your e-mail will appear in tomorrow's morning paper on the front page for the world to see: How would you feel about that?

For e-mail communication that is truly professional, remember:

- E-mail recipients ask two immediate questions when they see your e-mail: What is this, and what does it have to do with me? The faster you address those two questions (in the subject line) the greater the chance of your e-mail being read and attended to.

- E-mail is no place for an emotional discussion, especially a negative one. As soon as you pick up a problem, pick up the phone; don't e-mail.

- Copy only those who need to know. As much as possible, solve your own problems before your boss even knows there is a problem.

- Keep e-mails short and focused. Few e-mails over two hundred words will be read completely.

- Don't pass along Internet jokes or chain e-mails at work. We don't recommend you do it on your private e-mail either, but certainly not at work. All business e-mail accounts should be considered monitored.

> - Use the drafts folder often. Write, send it to drafts, then look at it again later. Any edits you can make for clarity?

One thing that will always be the same with any communication is how you connected with the other person. Keep this in the forefront of your mind at all times. Connection is what others really remember about you.

When presenting one-to-one in a more informal setting, I also use questions to provoke a discussion that demonstrates my knowledge and intellect. Phone presentations are actually easier because you can focus on your voice and the content—no one knows how old you are or what you look like!
Tammy Bratton, PharmD
Director, Regional Medical Liaisons
Amgen, Inc.

37

Planes, Trains, and Automobiles

At one time or another, you will travel for business purposes as well as for fun! Travel presents myriad opportunities for the savvy female networker. You're surrounded
by those you don't know well—most often in public places.
What could be more conducive to making connections?
Whether you travel on planes, trains, elevated trains, sub-
ways, buses, or automobiles, you can wisely use your travel
time to grow as a person, a communicator, and a presenter.

Ya Never Know

The person in the seat next to you on the subway may be the
person who connects you to a new client or even a new career. Great connections start small. A friend of ours was
about to bury herself in her favorite novel when her seatmate on the plane asked what she did for a living. Grudg-
ingly, she replied that she was a consultant, the conversation
continued, and she discovered she was talking to a newspaper columnist—the very one who later plugged her new
book in his column. She received many inquiries as a result
of that happenstance meeting. Ya never know where a conversation with a seatmate will take you. Of course, you need
to be cautious, but if the signs are right, your gut tells you it's

okay, and you can stow that e-book for a few minutes, start a conversation! Some good openers are, "Headed home?" or "Long day?" or "How do you like that book? I've heard a lot about it."

Plan Ahead for Cultural Differences

Engage your natural curiosity for people, places, and all things cultural. Being a good listener here is paramount, as is being a good question-asker. Be cognizant of what·lies ahead in terms of your global awareness. Every country, every state, every ethnic group has a great deal to teach us. Learn as much as you can before, during, and after your trip. It will all come in handy as you communicate with your fellow travelers, your hospitality contacts, and your business associates. Study the countries you'll visit. Even study the region or area you'll visit. You will find clues for conversation and for making a good impression. Familiarize yourself with local sports teams or attractions. You can always ask questions about them, if you can start with something like, "Is this really where the Cubs do their spring training?" or "Did da Vinci begin painting here?" Make note of what you learn, and journal for the present and the future. Your experience can be a real treasure for you someday.

Be Cautious with Food and Drink

With a fair amount of caution, be open to what happens and who you meet. There are many good people on the road, so be alert, stay in public places, and watch your alcohol intake. Consider not drinking alcohol or strictly limiting yourself to one wine or beer only. Eat lighter than usual on a trip, especially when you are with clients or your colleagues. This is no time to "let loose." Business continues 24-7 on a trip. Never get caught in the conference-goers trap of overindulgence away from home; the rumor mill loves a good conference late-night story. Make sure you're not the main character.

Reduce Your Stress

Those who travel well with energy to spare learn simple ways to reduce their stress on the road. For example, take the earlier plane for some alone time and more "on" time. No rushing means a clearer head when weather cancels planes and things change. Give yourself the comfort of less tense times. Rise a bit earlier than need be, and simply think rather than do. What will this day afford you the opportunity to accomplish beyond your to-do list? Eat less, exercise a bit more, and establish a routine for yourself. Even unpacking should have regularity to it so that there is no last-minute forgetting. Consider noise-reducing headphones for privacy as well as for music. They come in very handy when you don't want to talk to your seatmate.

Ask yourself time-management guru Alan Lakein's key question, "What is the best use of my time right now?" Sometimes that may mean a nap on the plane! Join an airline club early in your career, even though it may mean several hundred dollars. When you divide the hours you'll be there over a year, it will become your best bargain, and it puts you in a place where the executives are.

You're Always "On"

Remember, you are still on, even among strangers. Be aware that you represent the company everywhere you go. Competitors might be in the seat ahead of you. Consider dressing

fashionably even when going casual or in coach. Cyndi
never wears jeans on the plane—even when on vacation—
because she meets too many potential clients—and often
runs into actual ones. She wants to be seen as a credible consultant, not a casual vacationer. You never know whom you
will meet, and you just might get that upgrade!

Use Extra Time to Network

Have a layover? Extra hours between meetings? Make re-
newed contact with others strategically by knowing who
is in what city, and see if you can reconnect with college
friends or business colleagues. Kevin is a master at this. He
keeps logs of students, former neighbors, clients, administrative assistants, and more. He is rarely without a lunch
partner when he travels because of his extra effort to stay in
touch. And he has a lot more fun, as well! Often those casual
friendly lunches turn into more business, though he never
enters into the meeting with that as an agenda.

Impress Your Boss

Travel will raise your profile with your boss and your boss's
boss. Share what you are learning with your boss, especially
what you are learning informally. Competitive intelligence,
regional trends, and field-office politics are points of information your boss may want to hear about.

If you saw the one-time-only Renoir exhibit in Philadel-
phia and so did your boss, imagine the conversation. If on
your trip to Anchorage you were able to get to Seward and
your boss's boss knew that because she, too, had been there,
what kind of conversation and memory of it for her would
that be? Anne Frank's home in Amsterdam, any museum in
Paris, shopping in Casablanca or on Rodeo Drive, all of

these are not only fun and broadening, but they are also useful hooks to connect with others in a one-of-a-kind way.

Don't Stop at Good-bye

Commence a never-ending network. The people you meet can someday be important to your career. Stay in touch with those closest to you. Phone calls, notes, and e-mails are all good ways to pass the time and to keep others aware of your schedule. How about an old-fashioned postcard every now and then? It will certainly get their attention in the company mailbox.

To make business travel work for you,

- Be open to conversation just about anywhere. If you feel safe and able to connect with someone, do so. Often the most casual beginnings lead to the most fitting clients you'll ever want to have.

- Make an extra effort to be stress free so you will have energy. That often means *not* following the crowd, but taking a break, napping, drinking water not alcohol, and going to bed early.

- Use what you learn in your conversations with your superiors. Those who travel are seen as worldly, smart, and aware of what's going on in the world. Be sure to let your boss know you're among that group.

I use being female to my advantage. I dress to a "T" each and every time, never sexy, but I am very well dressed and that makes a difference. I maintain eye contact, never flirtatiously, but to keep engaged with them.

I dress well and I carry myself well. This helps me get past the "looks" quickly, because if you are well dressed the audience moves on to finding out if you really have the data. This is when I really have to deliver, be on top of my game, and demonstrate my credibility. Yes, first impressions are important.

Marie-Chantal Simard, PhD
Regional Medical Advisor
Medical Affairs
Abbott
Montreal

38

It's Just Dinner—Or Is It?

Dinner with colleagues is a time for some real strategy from the start. With whom do you want to talk? When do you want to approach them, and how do you want to craft your message? This is a vital part of time away from the office. It is also a presentation time of sorts. Many people in business regard the business lunch or dinner as a time to "let your hair down" and relax. Successful leaders and presenters know that's far from the truth. In fact, they rely on the fact that many think of the meal as the time to let their hair down, and then they make decisions based on how the dinner partner thinks and interacts "off hours." While a meal is a time to relax, never relax so much that you lose sight of the fact that it's still a "business" meal. Likewise, a golf date with a customer is "business" golf, not golf with your best friends.

Be aware, be gracious, and be prepared. Treat the waitstaff with respect, treat mistakes with forgiveness, and treat your guest with honor. If dining with clients is new for you, consider taking a class in business etiquette. You'll get a good review of how to act, speak, and even how to eat at these corporate meals.

One of Kevin's clients took his team out to dinner and at the end of the meal said, "I cannot let any of you loose with customers here or in Europe. You all ate like you were at home or the hot dog stand! We are all going to get training to do this well." What did he see them do wrong? Napkins bunched up on a plate as the meal finished, rolls eaten whole, "pardon my reach" grabbing for salt and pepper, gulping of wine, using the wrong fork, being rude to the waitstaff, and gnawing T-bone steaks throughout the meal.

Not long after, he hired an expert in etiquette, and his group finished with a real meal at a fancy restaurant as their final exam! Now some eight years later, they still regard this among the most memorable training they had as a team. Etiquette is not just something well-mannered people do; it is a set of standards and rules that helps others feel comfortable. The last thing you want your guest to feel is uncomfortable with your behavior, however unintended. Better to learn from the experts.

One young female executive we know routinely drinks too much at dinner meetings. She is known by her colleagues as "a big drinker." The first question from many in the group the next morning is, "How'd Sally do last night?" The answer is frequently, "The question really is how is she doing this morning?" This impression undercuts her even when she is at work, sober and competent, and she's completely in the dark about it (and about the office talk of what she's like "off site"). She may be an alcoholic. She may be an alcohol abuser. She may just be immature or insecure. We don't know. What we do know is that she is not a strategic presenter of herself or her ideas because her behavior is not acceptable in the business social environment. Not only is it unacceptable, but it will also limit her significantly.

When it comes to dinner with colleagues and customers, always decide on a drink limit, if you're having any, and then nurse that for the entire night. Even one drink will alter your behavior. You won't see the difference, but others will. If you want to test this out, go to your next party and drink no alcohol and observe those who do. You will notice the changes immediately. Therefore, stay in control of yourself when you are away from the office with your colleagues and customers.

It is important to choose wisely where you sit at a large dinner meeting. We recommend that you sit right next to the person you most want to influence. Don't let his or her fame, fortune, or title keep you from finding a way to have access. Sit next to or near the person, go to the buffet line with him, and so on. It's a way to meet a key person who is harder or nearly impossible to get close to in the office.

When you do have access, make sure you "present" yourself in one or more of the following ways: positive (no complaints about the service or the chicken), friendly (genuine smiles), encouraging (statements that comment on the other person's strengths), and valuable (what you say is useful to the other person). If this is a dinner meeting and the boss presents, don't just say she did a good job. Be different. Say something like "May I tell you what I noticed about the audience during your speech?" Believe us, everyone you say this to will want to know what you know!

You'll notice plenty of small talk going around the table. Be open to it, and make sure you don't dominate it—a common unknown-to-self blunder that significantly lessens your influence. You will be remembered as a "great conversationalist" when you listen more than you speak! Whenever you engage in small talk, resist the temptation to be the star, or the funny one, or the smart one. Make others feel that they are. Connect your contribution with words like *and* rather than *but* and never, ever say, "If you think that is funny, let me tell you this one!" One-upmanship is certain death to your ability to influence. Ask yourself as he or she speaks, *What is important to this person? What is she really saying to me about herself? How can I engage with him?*

Kevin is woefully ignorant about sports. He has to be very careful at meetings when the conversation turns to sports. He doesn't want to look like an ignoramus or as if he is a pompous something else! So he turns on encouraging questions and uses sports as the metaphor for life. Instead of trying to contribute knowledge, he attempts depth. Once he was speaking to a woman who really knew her basketball. He said to her, "You really understand the sport, don't you?" She perked up and said with a laugh, "In my family, with my father, you'd better know basketball if you wanted any attention at all!" So Kevin naturally asked, "When did you first understand what the inner workings of basketball were all about?" This led to a conversation about a special coach and, of course, with the right finesse, to how she leads her work team. How can this kind of talk not score points— no matter how illiterate you are in the sports arena?

Many employers use meals as a way to interview you for the promotion they haven't told you about yet. As with all business, the assessment starts before you know it. From the moment you leave your home, be "on."

Last, and certainly not least, be kind to your servers, even if they are incompetent. How you treat your servers at dinner is the way everyone surmises you treat others— especially when you are under pressure. It is a telltale test that leaders use to understand you.

So, keep the following in mind at a dinner engagement:

- Remember to put yourself in the physical zone of those you most want to influence. That may mean attending late-evening dinners or early-morning breakfasts that you'd rather not stay up or get up for.

- All talk is both big and small. Pay attention to what it says about them, and pay attention to what you are saying as you listen.

- Always be kind to your servers—you want to make a good impression with your colleagues by proving that you know how to treat people.

I never ever mix alcohol with my job. Never. I will get a fruit drink just to make others feel comfortable.

Newer professionals sometimes discuss too much of their private lives. They tend to treat a coworker as a person, not as a colleague. I have my friends and I have my colleagues. These are two different groups. Too friendly at work is not professional.

Marie-Chantal Simard, PhD
Regional Medical Advisor
Medical Affairs
Abbott
Montreal

39

Give the Business Eulogy— Differently

When a fellow staff member dies, you may choose or be chosen to do a eulogy at the funeral. Be ready to speak about this person in warm tones and with deliberate words. Find compelling words that uniquely describe this person.

You're there to reminisce about your experiences with the individual and tell stories that illustrate his or her unique character. Men and women will hear those stories differently. Men prefer the story to have a quick point and an action item. Women like the feeling tone of the story, some natural humor, and a rich description. Women listen to the words, men to the plot. When you stay aware of these differences during your preparation and accommodate them during your eulogy, you will connect with the audience.

Go Beyond the Known

Consider the impact of the following story: "What you may not know about Jane is that once when we were in an evaluation meeting, every executive in the room wanted to fire a junior exec. Jane made a quiet and impassioned argument for this person staying under her guidance. I heard that she even said, 'I will take responsibility for her myself.' She was quite a woman. And she is the reason they didn't fire me that day! Thank you, Jane, you will always be in my fond memories." This story approach will help you in preparing the eulogy or memorial talk or even the mention of the deceased back at the office.

When you go beyond the known, you inform everyone, those "in the know" and those who are on the periphery of that person's business or family life. The purpose is to bring the community there together. While we honor those who died, funerals and eulogies are not for them—they are for the living. Once again, keep your focus on the audience. When you focus your comments on the deceased, your eulogy will lose impact because it will appear "too personal" or "too intimate" and will make the audience uncomfortable.

The Magic of the Story

Stories capture our total being. Ministers, rabbis, and priests have known this for years. When the congregation's attention is wandering, they pull out a story, and just like four-year-olds, we all give them our undivided attention. Therefore, don't be afraid to tell stories with humor, with poignancy, with strong descriptive words, and with enough emotion for the audience to hear. This can be a touchy balance. Your eulogy can have emotion without becoming emotional. Practice your eulogy, especially the tough parts. If you choke up or cry, just pause. Audiences will allow you to gather your feelings and proceed. Sometimes a coworker or family member will come to your rescue and want to take over at the pulpit. If they do, and if you want to continue, simply grasp his or her hand and say, "Please stay here with me while I finish." This gives the person a role and makes it clear that you don't want to be rescued.

Certainly while you'll have plenty of stories to choose from, be careful to respect the privacy of the individual.

Choose stories that capture and inspire, stories that are fun but that don't make fun, and stories that are clearly positive in nature. In short, make your story one everyone can relate to—true, interesting, informative, and real.

When you are preparing to give a eulogy for a coworker,

- Understand your critical leadership role when it comes to death, disease, and the suffering of your coworkers. Be there for them in the hospital, at the wake, and at the service, and you will capture a unique moment in time.

- Understand the power of the story. Don't be afraid to get personal and to talk openly about impact.

- Take the initiative when you are intersecting the lives of those you work with. They may hold back, but leaders cannot afford to be reticent.

When relaying bad news to someone, be respectful of the person and their privacy.

If discussing a person who's been terminated, simply say that effective today, this person is no longer with us and this other person is in charge. Don't engage in gossip—it makes you look bad and creates anxiety in the organization.

When bad things happen, don't complain—move on. You may be a loss to the group/company if you are asked to leave, but a complainer is often an ongoing loss for an organization if a boss is willing to endure that behavior.

Jeri Stewart, MS, RN
National Director
Clinical Science Managers
Abbott Immunology

40

Influence on Retreat

Your retreat leader has a goal. Help her reach that goal by listening to the wording of it, by analyzing the topics covered in the retreat, and by looking at who's been invited. Everything fits together to create the big picture. No component has been random. If you aren't sure where you fit in, find out beforehand. Ask what you can bring with you to make the best of your time.

Because you are female, your tendency is to try to listen. Don't feel you have to take on that responsibility for everyone. Cyndi once led a presentations class in a retreatlike atmosphere and asked the largely male crowd to complete some slide work that night. The next day, only the woman had hers done; the guys said they hadn't understood. Who knows? Maybe they didn't. Cyndi still remembers the look on the woman's face and what she said: "Oh, come on. I was up all night with these. I accidentally erased the first file, and I had to redo it. And these guys didn't even do it!"

Make sure you're not taking on the work of the guys. Do your part—but *only* your part.

Use Retreat Time Wisely

Some great and very close relationships can be built at away-from-work events. We both have several lifelong friends whom we see only at National Speakers Association meetings. But just because you're in casual dress and not at work, that doesn't mean it's all play. Get to know people on the breaks, and ask them different questions than you might at work. Perhaps you've always wanted to know more about the college they went to or the town where they grew up. Feel free to ask questions like this at retreats—it is a time to get to know people on a slightly more personal level.

Always ask first, and talk about yourself second. You are influencing and making an impression. You are mingling and may need that person in the future to complete a picture or champion an idea. Cyndi met a manager named Nancy at a telemarketing association meeting years ago who went on to become her best champion—simply because Nancy didn't know anyone else who did what Cyndi does! She knew only telemarketing and recognized Cyndi as a resource.

Reveal the Heart

We once facilitated a retreat with the executive team of a multimillion-dollar company, including the president. The team was a blend of executives from two companies—diverse in age and background and trained in two different cultures. After working through a morning of interpersonal-style discussion, culture definition, and goal setting, the female president made a very important statement to the group of men. She said, "I just want to know if you're on my team—if you are with me."

She had, in one sentence, revealed the heart of the discussion. While the morning had been poignant and productive, it was not until after this statement that the men revealed their significant fears based on the past. By revealing the heart, the president opened the floor even further to airing conflict and clearing expectations.

Women are particularly good at this. Remember this story the next time you are reluctant to get at "the elephant in the room"—the unspoken or hidden agenda. Do it! Most people, especially younger generations, will appreciate your honesty.

Dinner Directions

Kevin networks at meals—breakfast, lunch, or dinner. If he has a free day or partial day, you can just about bet that he is taking someone out to eat. Close relationships that begin over a meal will grow over time. When you do take a meal with someone, strive to make it less about business and more about them. Memories of the meal and your time together are what the agenda is really about.

When you're out of the office, on retreat, or at a meeting, think carefully about whom you will dine with. Don't give in to the "best friend syndrome" every time. Invite someone new, and learn about him or her. They may become a key person in your network. Do this especially with those who can stop your project, who can make life difficult for your team—even an enemy! When you know someone else and they know you apart from your work agenda, it is very difficult to continue to be "difficult."

Cyndi likes to host dinners at her home. She builds lasting relationships with colleagues and clients that way. She enjoys learning new tidbits about colleagues or acquaintances away from the office. She keeps the parties fairly small so that conversation is easy and everyone meets everyone fully.

The point to all this talk about food is that as it nourishes our bodies, it also nourishes our relationships.

When on a retreat,

- Advance your network.

- Advance your listening.

- Advance your list of dining partners.

Women are not listened to in the same way men listen to men. There are more sidebar conversations when a woman presents than when a man does.

Ultimately, the audience decides whether or not they will listen to a presentation and whether or not they will use it.

Carolyn Hope Smeltzer, RN, EdD
PricewaterhouseCoopers

Frequently Asked Questions

How can I improve my behavior at meetings and be taken more seriously?

Definitely do *not* fetch the coffee unless you drew the short straw! Do *not* take notes, and if asked, say you prefer not to . . . today. Be sure to add the word *today,* as this softens your refusal. You don't want to appear to be an iron lady. Do *not* talk about your children unless asked, and then answer in one sentence—unless it's a sporting event. Then you can use two. The details can make you or break you. Be sure they make you.

Why are some speakers so well liked they can give a terrible talk and still receive rave reviews—and the rest of us have to work very, very hard just to get by?

Life is not fair, but you can continue to improve and get better so that you start receiving rave reviews! The bottom line is that some people have lots of charisma and connecting power, and the rest of us just have less of it. Comparing is a dangerous game and a trap that you don't want to fall into. Simply do what you do, and let others do what they do. Keep building your speaking skills, and stop worrying about others who have an advantage for reasons that have nothing to do with you.

I have a new boss who is a "nuts-and-bolts results" kind of person. I need ideas for my first large group presentation with

the boss in attendance. Do I have to ditch my softer approach, which is really more me?

As long as the boss hired you, kept you, and works well with you, don't change too much—apparently you are a value to the boss just the way you are. That being said, consider adding rather than subtracting from or changing your style. First and always, add more preparation to your presentations, especially when the boss is present. Second, get to the meat of your presentation quickly and then present details from that. The meat is the theme, the "it" of your presentation. Third, add plenty of "and the reason this is important is because . . ." to your presentation. Go for benefits and what you want them to know and conclude. Don't wait for the audience to conclude on their own. Fourth, have a strong summary conclusion that is fact and action based. Fifth, get immediate feedback from your boss so you can learn what, if anything, you should improve upon for next time. Keep your communication efficient and concise. And remember, the reason you are still there is because the boss likes you and finds you to be of value to the company.

I'll be leading a meeting where there are mostly women and perhaps a few men. Any suggestions?

We were once at an organizational retreat where twenty of the twenty-two members were women. The organizer made clear in her opening speech that all contributions were of value, and she welcomed the two men as groundbreakers and pioneers in the movement. She had welcomed them with affirmation not exclusion. She chose to welcome them with affirmation rather than to treat them as a segment of the group who were too few in number to make valuable contributions. She demonstrated her awareness of the differences present and made them feel like equals. Throughout the retreat, the two men in the group spoke up confidently and voiced their opinions. The organizer continued to reward them with her awareness and her appreciation, making sure they were heard, understood, and empathized with. Everyone was treated with respect and was given fair time to speak.

I notice sometimes that members of the audience are not very engaged in what I'm saying. They are just staring at me, and sometimes not even laughing when others are. It is very distracting for me. Any ideas for how I can stop being so distracted?

Don't look at them. Look first to those who are engaged with you, and then ramp it up a bit. Walk over to the section in the audience that seems less interested, smile a bit more, raise your volume, and move them into groups of two or three briefly to discuss a question to charge up the format of the talk a little bit. These nonengaged folks may be tired, worried, and distracted. It is up to you to get them back on track.

I see other speakers emphasizing certain words for impact. How do they know which words to emphasize?

They are verbally punctuating their message, which is a very effective technique. They punch up words to help sell their idea—words that build toward the theme or reason they're speaking. For example, *goal* or *win* or *success* are words that are often emphasized, but in your world, the words could be whatever resonates with the audience. To emphasize correctly, select key words and use greater volume and eyes that connect. All of this relays the core message back to the audience about what is important.

I work in government, and my female boss has coached me to dress and act as the men do. Her exact words have been, "It's about being 'one of the guys.' That's what success is here." I don't feel this is me, yet I can't afford to walk away from this

entry-level position, because the benefits are great and I like the work overall.

Modify what "being one of the guys" would look like for you. Perhaps wear the blue, black, or gray suits that your boss wears, but add a touch of your own style with a more feminine blouse. Keep your hair, shoes, and nails conservative, and be a "guy's guy" by being assertive and to the point. But keep your own sense of humor, smile, and ability to empathize. Watch what works for you and what doesn't. You'll be surprised to discover that you will be successful at work without taking your boss's bit of advice quite so literally.

How can I dress for success when I make under forty thousand a year?

Guess what? Most of us began our careers that way! Elicit the help of an experienced salesclerk at one of the larger department stores that has seasonal sales. Buy plain-colored pants and skirts that are modestly priced; put your money into nice, well-tailored jackets. You can hide an inexpensive blouse under a more expensive jacket. The discount designer outlets are great places for new professionals if you don't mind shopping a season or two behind the trends. Discount chain stores that carry off-season designer clothing are great places to find shirts, simple blouses, and jewelry. Just make sure nothing is see-through or gaudy.

Should I begin my talk with customary thank-yous or get right into the presentation?

We recommend that you always begin with the meat or something for the audience to chew on as substantial and interesting. You can always thank throughout your presentation, which is a nice twist. Simply tie the thank-you and the recipient into the point you're addressing at the moment, for example, "We've made great headway this year with our volunteers. Sheila, thank you especially for your leadership in this area."

What modifications do I make to my presentation if there are children in the audience? Funerals, weddings, and even some of my off-site business meetings have children present.

Recognize them, but don't pander to them. Children can spot a phony at twenty paces. If it is an adult affair, stay the course. If it is a family affair, incorporate some child references, but don't change your voice to a squeaky one or make yourself sound silly. Children like it when you speak "up" to them rather than "down" to them. You may want to consider adding a few visuals with movement that reference current TV stars, technology, or rock artists, as long as they fit with your point. Today's children perk up with technology and movement.

I'm a thirty-something-year-old newly promoted director in my organization with mostly older women reporting to me. I need to address them for the first time in my new role. Help!

Women in the baby boomer generation (born 1943 to 1960) and veteran generation (born 1922 to 1943) like to be heard and given praise; they enjoy face-to-face discussion and interaction more than your generation typically does. Try beginning with a short statement honoring them as a great team. Immediately go around and ask them each a simple question such as, "What team accomplishment are you most proud of?" or "What are you most proud of to date?" Then thank them for their input, and offer the group three of your ideas for the future. Encourage them to contact you at any time, and take the first follow-up step by sending each individual an e-mail with some positive comments and best wishes moving forward.

Why is it so hard to present to my peers?

We're setting ourselves up for it! Sociologist Leon Fes-
tinger (1954) had a theory about this: We seek out others
like us for a means of social comparison. The theory suggests that people judge themselves largely in comparison to
others. Do you want to know if you are attractive, popular,
healthy, or smart? The only answer may be in how you perceive the way you stack up to the people around you. Social
comparison can be useful when it enhances self-esteem or
serves as the basis for reasonable self-improvement. However, it can encourage dysfunction when the comparison es-
tablishes an unrealistic standard. The next time you present
to peers, remind yourself that your peers help you to figure
out where you still need to grow and where you're performing up to par.

When I disagree significantly with the speaker before me, what do I say or not say?

Find an area of agreement first, even if it means simply
complimenting his or her passion for the subject matter.
Then simply say, "I have a slightly different viewpoint, and
I look forward to finding a way to meet this challenge effectively regardless of our different perspectives." When you
can, compliment him or her for anything said that is of interest and support to the overall cause. As you finish your
presentation, provide an action item that includes the person in discussions about the issue at hand.

Occasionally I need to present with a colleague who is very energetic and fun but sometimes he is too loud and overly dramatic. We work with larger groups when two presenters are needed. How can I work effectively with this person?

Chances are he is overcompensating for some fear or anxiety he feels when in front of a group. Why not tape your-
selves sometime and play it back together? Compliment him

on his energy; perhaps suggest other ways that he can shine (writing on the flipchart, paraphrasing only, etc.). Talk about how you might work better as a team. Also, own up to your own faults in front of a group and ask him to help you as well. When you're in front of the group again, use humor when he turns his excitement on unexpectedly. You could say, "Wow what a delivery, Mike. I think we're all awake now!"

When I make presentations to my managers and my customers, I often find myself feeling emotional—sometimes defensive or overly excited. How should I control this?

By all means, use emotion to connect with your audience; this is different from becoming "emotional" during your presentation. Especially because you are a woman, skillfully use emotion, not emotionalism. Using emotion with skill means that you are able to convey from the inside out—the importance, the depth, and the need for action or even new consideration of your topic. Being emotional in the bad sense of the word means that you are allowing inner feelings to spill out into your content and your interaction in an unfiltered, unreasonable way. We often try to keep our emotion too much on the inside, as we observed when a pharmaceutical executive who was watching one of our coaching sessions for a skilled female on his staff said to her afterwards, "If you had any feeling for that presentation, I want you to know that I didn't detect a note of it." As you craft the content of your presentation, be aware of the emotion that goes with that content. Have the courage in your business meetings to use emotion without being emotional. When you are angered by an audience comment, think before you speak. Instead of being defensive, say something like: "You must have a good reason for saying that. May I ask you what it is?" or "I appreciate the idea you have; I am suggesting something different." Always, always use emotion to influence, not to vent.

I'm attending a conference for the first time with my sales team, and I have been asked to introduce my mentor. I want to do a stellar job. Do you have any suggestions?

Good for you! A great introduction is practiced, professional, and personal. Know your opening perfectly, and try to go beyond the typical "It gives me great pleasure to introduce . . ." opening. Instead, think of some personal anecdote that your mentor will cherish. For example, "When I first did a drive-along in the car to key accounts with Sandy Moore, I was so impressed, I took twenty-five pages of notes. Sandy really knows how to manage those accounts. I don't know how she does it along with four little boys under twelve, but she does a great job. I am honored to introduce my mentor and our next speaker, Sandy Moore, Director of Key Account Sales." Note that you should use a unique first line, a key professional credit, and a clever personal tie-in to her topic.

Please give me some tips on how to deal with the "good ole boys" that still remain at my workplace.

Unfortunately older men will sometimes call you "the little lady from headquarters" or say you're "lookin' mighty good today, darlin'." None of this is okay, but be ready for it with more than a sneer. Sometimes men use these phrases as a test to see how you'll react. If you fight it, you may wind up as if you are fighting with your five-year-old in the grocery store. You will lose. (Actually both events have lots in common—publicity, immaturity, and vulnerability!) One of our clients says she handles what she calls the "good ole boy syndrome" by dealing with them one on one and finding out what their key important issues are. She shows them her knowledge and value, and she stays in close touch with them, asking for their advice and help as needed. Understand that you can find many other ways to respond that do not have to be reactive. It is also perfectly okay to say to them in privacy, "Tom, I enjoy working with you, but nobody calls me darlin' but my dad."

Or even, "Joe, I learn a lot from going on sales calls with you, but when you called me 'the little lady from headquarters' in front of Mr. Jones, I was embarrassed." Notice that you start with an ego stroke—a sincere one—and finish with your feeling. This should encourage them to apologize and offer any additional explanation.

How can I encourage honest feedback about my presentation skills from my audience and from my boss?

Ask the right questions. Then listen, but listen only to the right feedback. The right questions have to do with your objective and the effectiveness of your presentation. If the audience knows what you spoke about and if they feel you were effective, then you are in the clear! The right feedback should come first from the person who asked you to speak. If he or she is not happy or has a concern, address their concerns immediately. The next important person to consult with is yourself—how do you feel you did? What could you improve next time? Sometimes our audiences don't see what we see, and that is okay. If we can correct it for next time, all the better. Then there will be comments from the audience. Be careful here. Some people will love you no matter what, and some will not like you no matter what. However, certain critiques are important to pay attention to. For example, an audience member may say, "I didn't quite understand when you—," or "At times it was difficult to hear you," or "You seemed to be speaking only to the left side of the room." These can be very helpful comments to hear. Judgmental comments ("You didn't look like your picture. I don't agree with anyone from the South. Your suit didn't seem to fit. You certainly enjoyed yourself more than we did. I didn't want to come here today anyway.") will hurt and they won't help you to improve. You must learn to let go of that type of critical feedback.

A quick surefire way to improve is when you are complimented, you say, "Thank you very much. What did you like especially?" What they say next is the connective piece.

I had to present spontaneously without notice because a presenter didn't show. I wasn't happy that I had to do it nor was I pleased with my performance. Any advice for next time this happens?

Always prepare. We always prepare something to say for every breakfast, lunch, dinner, and business meeting we go to, even if the chance of having to speak is remote. You can also have a general formula in your head like many politicians and CEOs do. (Meat of your message—thank—observe—ask—request—thank—then sit!) You might say, "Our industry is facing a challenge of enormous proportions. If you saw today's *Wall Street Journal,* you know that," or "I want to first thank Brenda for her excellent presentation on—," or "What I have noticed," or "And so I have three questions for us today," or "My request is that we act quickly and deliberatively," or "May I say thank you again to—" Having this outline in your head will help you to pull off the spontaneous presentation. One thing to never, ever do is refuse the invitation to speak. It makes you look suspicious, incompetent, or timid, none of which you want to appear to be. Also, always at least glance at page one of the *Wall Street Journal, USA Today, The New York Times,* or the local paper from the city you are in before you go to your meeting. You will always find an article that can relate in some way to your audience.

My firm is very big on presentation skills. How can I improve with each successive talk?

Try this technique: evaluate, educate, and innovate. Evaluations from others help if you read them carefully and nondefensively. Not all of them will help, but one or two will routinely help greatly. Give the evaluator room to write and not just rate you on a numerical scale. Another way to evaluate is to audio-record every presentation and then listen to it. This way, you are self-educating, which can be very helpful as well. Educate yourself by reading and by joining Toastmasters (www.toastmasters.org), which is a great way to receive constructive and encouraging feedback regularly. Finally, innovate by putting something new in each presentation. Professional comedians do this to test new material. You can do the same; innovate to stay fresh and interesting. Your audience will take notice and stay alert.

Can I tell the same story to the same group if it has been a year or so since they heard me?

If it is a good story, you sure can. The nice thing about audiences is that they forget about 90 percent of what you said immediately after you say it! Audiences are more likely to remember a personal story, but they usually like hearing it again! We encourage you to develop more stories so that you will be known as "the storyteller" when you show up to your meetings. Your audiences will look forward to hearing you speak each and every time because they know you are interesting and can engage the group.

When I present, I sometimes feel like a teacher, other times like an entertainer. Who am I supposed to be?

Both are fine, depending on the audience. Be animated, interested, and show your passion for the topic. Also teach like the best teacher you ever had. Don't try to be eloquent so much as effective. Don't go for perfection at the expense of providing useful information. Don't try to be funny.

Instead, enjoy the natural humor that will flow from audience participation, storytelling, and personal anecdotes.

I frequently meet business people on airplanes who may very well be my future clients. Do you have any ideas for me when I am presenting to seatmate 21A from 21B?

Yes, recognize everyone as a potential client. Kevin was sitting next to a young man on a flight and asked, "What line of work are you in?" The young man replied, "Investment banking," with a bored expression. Kevin persisted with his typical follow-up question that almost always engages: "Did you go to school to learn how to do that?" The reply, "No." Kevin gave it one more shot. "Can you tell me a little about your work?" The killer reply came, "Oh, lots of money stuff." Now, Kevin could have been a potential customer for this young man, a network of referrals, and even an interesting conversationalist. All was lost because the young man thought his potential clients were on the ground, not right next to him. Treat every seatmate as a potential client or colleague, and see what happens.

I am an administrative assistant to a VP, and she wants me to give an update to the CEO. I am a pretty good presenter, but this one makes me nervous. Do you have any advice?

Nerves can be a good thing! They keep us on alert and encourage us to be well prepared. Collaborate with your boss. Remember, preparation is the key to success. Know the objectives of the meeting clearly, stick to your time constraints, and consider treating the CEO as a real person, not just as a title. Some CEOs will interrupt you with a question. They do this not to be rude but because they get an idea and need an answer immediately. Never say, "Oh, I'll be getting to that slide in a little bit." Finally, remember to throw the meat out first, quicken your pace, simplify your message, don't belabor what they already know, and smile.

I have good news to present to my firm, but it involves a major reorganization. I anticipate that some people may be upset. Do you have any ideas for how best to approach the topic?

Get buy-in from the most important executives, especially the ones it will affect the most. Show them what you are going to say, and ask their advice. Take your time here. They are your most important audience. Then, frame the context, make the announcement, reassure the audience immediately on what this means to their job. ("This is a development realignment only; no one is losing their job over this.") Then arrange for them to go into break out groups with three short questions and then bring them back for report outs and Q & A. I saw one leader do this, and it was a terrific way for her to announce and then manage the announcement. (The formula to follow is: Prepare—Be Succinct—Reassure—Provide Time for Response.)

I am an introvert. How can I speak up effectively during group meetings?

True introverts make some of the best listeners. Work on three or four great icebreaker questions, and they'll carry you through the most difficult opening moments of the meeting, the coffee break, or the dinner meeting.

I'm fine for the first twenty to thirty minutes at business dinners. It's the longer ones where I'm stuck in one seat at a long table for three hours that test my conversation and tolerance skills. Any ideas on how to make the best of it?

We've all been there—especially at conference gatherings away from home. First, tell yourself you're in it for the long haul—not the sprint. It's a different mind-set. Explore topics with your seatmates in more detail. Change topics more slowly, and don't exhaust yourself conversationally. Feel free to stand and stretch and move to someone around the table to chat for a few moments. Connect the two people on either side of you in conversation with each other and with you so that you can take conversation breaks to just listen to them. Allowing others the spotlight will help conserve your energy for long nights of conversation.

How long is too long for a presentation?

One minute longer than the audience can bear! End on time or early every time if only by a few minutes. Leave your audience wanting more. The attention span of an audience member is about ten to twelve minutes; so don't lecture longer than that without some change in format, interaction, Q & A, facilitation, small group activity, or stories and humor (never a joke!). Keep in mind this adage of unknown origin: "A good speech has a good beginning and a good ending, both of which are kept very close together."

I once called a board meeting to which everyone arrived late except the administrative assistant and me. I was hesitant to scold. Next time, should I?

To scold is probably not the right attitude for you to have at this point. To make others honestly aware is. This tardy behavior must be recognized, and a good time to do that is before the meeting ends. Say something like, "Most of you had difficulty arriving on time today. Is there anything we should all be aware of for next time?" This happened to Kevin, and as annoyed as he was, he asked the question anyway. It turns out the company shuttle bus had broken down. He had wanted to lecture, but was glad he didn't!

My sales manager tells me to work on my monotone and diction when I present, but when I try to do something different, I don't feel natural. Any suggestions?

Joan Sparks, who has been a Chicago-based voiceover talent agent for twenty-five years, has heard thousands of female voices. Joan is an expert on recognizing natural vocal characteristics and talent, and also recognizing when voices need help. She told us that vocal quality is definitely a part of a person's charisma. (In fact, in her industry she's noticed that a natural sound is in demand by her ad agency clients, as opposed to the more "produced" sound of the past.) However, to be natural at the expense of being understood and believed is another thing. The best way to hear your voice as others do is to record it, recognize how you sound, and work with a coach to help you use word color, emphasis, and variety in your presentations. On a final note, Joan told us that she has noticed another trend—increased mumbling by young people, especially young women. She encourages young women to articulate and project—even when on a microphone. It sounds like your sales manager wants you to do the same.

What if there is a meeting in my large boardroom right before mine? How can I take the control you want me to take with the room and the opening?

That's quite a common circumstance. Enlist your participants to help you. When you walk in to find a poor setup or lighting, simply ask them to move chairs or call the audiovisual department. When you need help, Speak Up!

Top Ten Tips

1. Look the part, right from the start.

Your professional dress, hair, handshake, and handouts will set up that you mean business. For women, pants and a jacket with a conservative line and a firm lapel are optimal. This choice allows you to move just about anywhere, use a mike if needed—the firm lapel works well for lavaliere microphones—and yet maintain your style and femininity. Show your individuality with a bright color, simple jewelry, and well-groomed hair. Always wear a jacket of some kind (casual or formal, depending) to the presentation; you can opt to take it off if needed. The reason this is our first tip is because it is the first thing the audience will see. They will naturally and immediately make decisions about who you are by how you look.

2. Really, really think through your opening.

All speakers say, "Thank you for coming." Beginning with something more meaningful will signal that you want to get right to business—that you are valuable and worth listening to. For example, "The retail garment business today is not about fashion and design; it is about the perceived fashion design of our value interpreters—our customers. We don't need more designers; we need more understanding of customer mind-set" is a much better opening than "Today I am going to talk to you about retail sales this quarter." Show them that you thoughtfully considered your approach and that you mean business. In other words, throw them some meat to chew on.

3. Involve the group ASAP.

This doesn't mean you have to have them sprinting around the room and coloring on flip charts, but it does mean you need to break them out of passive mode and into active mode. Ask them questions, ask for a show of hands, pass out a startling handout, ask them to comment on something. Take a risk, and have them meet in groups of two or three to discuss a focus question. This is really no risk at all. Our experience is that all audiences love it. They like to talk! When you involve them, you accomplish two purposes: You connect them to you, and you manage your nervousness. When someone else is talking, the focus is now away from you, and you can listen and tie in what they say to your next point. Be sure to bring name tags. First names only in large marker print are best.

4. Don't fall into the "too much, too fast, too apologetic" trap.

If the meeting is running late or questions begin to take too much time, don't try to squeeze it all in. Focus on what you think they'll be most interested in, and then show only those slides that are most important. Without apology, give the fifteen-minute version of your hourlong talk (which you always prepare for just in case) and make no mention of running short on time. Answer any questions briefly, and keep the pace moving. Their questions are almost always more important than what you planned to say, anyway, so consider it an honor if you get a lot. It means they are interested and involved and that you are of high value to them.

5. Most of the time, *three* points is enough.

Give up your female eye for details and when presenting. Lead your group toward thinking in threes. "When I speak to new hires, three important things come to mind." Or "I see three keys to the successful future direction of this department." Speaking in threes allows your audience to remember the most important items and details. Ancient Celtic horsemen traveled in threes to conquer invaders. Three is a timeworn concept of unity and support. Two is somehow not enough, and more than three is hard to remember. Be memorable!

6. Be heard, literally and figuratively.

How often have you heard someone say, "Speak up!" at a meeting? Make sure this is not directed to you. Punch out your words with emphasis and volume. Combine strong eye contact with your increased volume. If you have been asked to speak up, make sure you increase your volume for the rest of the meeting. Rarely do presenters or contributors speak too loudly! No matter how right you are, if you speak softly, you increase the chances of your opinion being disregarded. Speak from your strength with volume.

7. Use your natural style with strength.

Be yourself—but with the adjustment of knowing your strength and the perceived need of the audience. Yes, you might be a detail person, but the audience needs the big picture also. Yes, you might be nonconfrontational, but the audience needs to hear your conviction. And yes, you may be perfect in many ways, but the audience will feel better if you don't come across as perfect. Psychiatrist Dr. Rudolf Dreikurs recommended, "Have the courage to be imperfect" in approaching others. When you move away from a perfection mentality, you can move to a mind-set focused on usefulness rather than on what is right and wrong.

8. Be responsive, not defensive.

Be very careful of appearing defensive when you present. Even if your data or your ideas are attacked, it is critical that you respond rather than react. Responding means asking clarifying questions such as, "What specific point are you addressing?" "Can you help me understand why you feel so strongly?" When you say "I disagree," "You're wrong," "That's crazy," "You've got to be kidding," you are vulnerable to more attacks and, more important, less useful to the audience.

9. Take and ask for every opportunity to present.

Never refuse an opportunity to speak about what you know, even if it makes you nervous. You certainly do not want to accept any invitation to present about something that you do not know. You do want to gain valuable experience by presenting about your expertise. When you are invited, it is usually a compliment to your value. Even if you are nervous, speak. The experience, the exposure, and the education are well worth it.

10. Have the courage to think about the audience and not about you.

This is the key to every presenter's success, but few actually know about it. When you focus on yourself, the audience can sense it and your presentation will look like a show about you. Sometimes that will work. However, when you focus on them, the audience knows intuitively that you are special, which is a greater achievement. They trust that you are creating a learning environment and that they will walk away with something that benefits them rather than simply a memory of a performance. Think *them*!

> *Memorable women presenters seem warm to me. Some express warmth in the form of humor geared toward the audience; some show this in specific connections with audience members; others engage the crowd with their eyes—making expressive eye contact throughout the presentation in accord with various important points. Self-assurance stands out to me, as well. I also remember those women who made me realize that someone of any age, gender, or socioeconomic background could have made the same speech.*
> Erin McKinney, JD

Helpful Resources

Arbinger Institute. *Leadership and Self Deception*, 2002.
This book has a unique approach to leadership.

Aristotle. *The Art of Rhetoric*, trans. H. C. Lawson-Tancred.
New York: Penguin Books, 1991.
The chapter on persuasion is a must-read for all speakers.

Buzan, Tony. *The Mind Map Book*. New York: Penguin
Books, 1996.
*A remarkable book and approach that could well change the way
you think about and interact with teams, ideas, and innovations.*

Campbell, Susan. *Saying What's Real: 7 Keys to Authentic
Communication and Relationship Success*. Novato, CA: HJ
Kramer, 2005.
*A very good resource to help you through conflict, and a quick
read.*

Carnegie, Dale. *How to Win Friends and Influence People*.
New York: Pocket Books, 1990.
*A classic. And it was written before any of us were born!
After seventy years, this is the one book that your boss has
read—as has her boss, and hers before that. If you read only
one book on leadership, this is the one.*

Gladwell, Malcolm. *Blink: The Power of Thinking Without Thinking*. Backbay Books, 2005.
  About the decisive glance that knows in an instant. Gladwell campaigns for snap judgments and mind-reading.

———. *The Tipping Point*. New York: Little Brown, 2002.
  A must-read for all who want to think differently about new ideas.

Johansson, Frans. *The Medici Effect*. Boston: Harvard Business School Publishing, 2004.
  This book covers creativity, innovation, and more.

Kawasaki, Guy. *The Art of the Start*. New York: Penguin Books, 2004.
  Written from an entrepreneur's business point of view, this book has many applications for self-improvement.

Lyerly, Barry, and Maxey, Cyndi. *Training from the Heart: Developing Your Natural Training Abilities to Inspire the Learner and Drive Performance on the Job*. Alexandria, VA: ASTD Press, 2000.
  Geared for those who train and develop others—either full-time or as part of their jobs. Shows how to find your style and encourage interaction.

Maxey, Cyndi, and Bremer, Jill. *It's Your Move: Dealing Yourself the Best Cards in Life and Work*. New Jersey: Financial Times/Prentice Hall, 2003.
  An innovative way to look at initiative and life change. There are chapters on etiquette, voice, speaking, and fashion.

McKenna, Patrick J., and Maister, David H. *First Among Equals*. New York: The Free Press, 2002.

An excellent resource for learning the ins and outs of professionals on a team.

Owen, Harrison. *Open Space Technology.* San Francisco: Berrett-Koehler Publishers, 1997.

Rosenberg, Marshall. *Non-violent Communication: A Language of Life.* Encinitas, CA: Puddledancer Press, 2003.
An excellent presentation of the human relations skills of effective communication.

Winters, Rita. *The Green Desert: A Silent Retreat.* New York: Crossroad Press, 2004.
A beautifully written introspective book by a former advertising executive who made a life change.

Two associations to develop your network and your skills:

For speaking practice and for growing your expertise in presenting, join Toastmasters, a nonprofit organization developing public speaking and leadership skills through practice and feedback in local clubs since 1924. Toastmasters Groups are in your area, some even at your workplace. To find meeting locations, go to www.toastmasters.org.

The National Speakers Association has chapters in your area as well as national meetings and conventions. To find your local chapter's location, go to www.nsaspeaker.org. NSA is the preeminent association for speakers, writers, and consultants who speak and present professionally.

Listen and watch classic speeches at www.americanrhetoric .com.

About the Authors

Cyndi Maxey, CSP (M.A., Communication Studies, Northwestern University), is a communication consultant and speaker specializing in communication that drives profitable performance. Cyndi holds a Certified Speaking Professional designation with the National Speakers Association, the group's highest earned designation, held by fewer than one hundred and ninety-five women internationally. She has owned and operated Maxey Creative, Inc., a communication consulting firm, since 1989. In addition to her seventy-five-plus published articles, Cyndi has coauthored four books: *Present Like a Pro* (St. Martin's Press, 2006), *It's Your Move: Dealing Yourself the Best Cards in Life and Work* (FT/Prentice Hall, 2003), *Training from the Heart: Developing Your Natural Abilities to Inspire the Learner and Drive Performance on the Job* (ASTD Books, 2000), and *The Communication Coach* (Coloring Outside the Lines, 1998). Having acted in many professional plays, commercials, voice-overs, and industrial films, she brings a strong performance background to her coaching and presentations. She lives and works in Chicago, Illinois, where her active family provides both balance and chaos in her life. Contact Cyndi at cmaxey@cyndimaxey.com or through www.cyndimaxey.com.

   Kevin E. O'Connor, CSP (M.A., Education, St. Xavier College; M.A., Counseling Psychology, Alfred Adler Institute; M.A., Spirituality, Loyola University), is a leadership consultant and professional speaker. He specializes in working with professionals (physicians, engineers, information technologists, dentists, nurses, and others) who have been promoted to positions where they now lead their former peers.

Since 1976, Kevin has spoken professionally more than eighty-five times per year on average. He coaches professionals around the country and teaches graduate students at Chicago's Loyola University and at Columbia College, Chicago's performing arts school. He has also taught at the Katholieke Universiteit in Leuven, Belgium, outside of Brussels.

Kevin is the author of three books: *A Handbook for Ministers of Care* (Liturgy Training Publications, 1997), *When All Else Fails: Finding Solutions to Your Most Persistent Management Problems* (1992, 1997), and *Profit-Ability: Leading Teams to a Better Bottom Line* (2002). He has coauthored *Present Like a Pro* (St. Martin's Press, 2006) and has contributed to *A Parents' Guide to Special Education for Children with Visual Impairments* (AFB Press, 2007), *Skills for Success: A Career Education Handbook for Children and Adolescents with Visual Impairments* (AFB Press, 1999), *Replenishing the Well: Insights and Inspiration for the Field of Visual Impairment* (Ozark Learning, 1997), and an as yet untitled and unpublished book on parenting and blindness (Hadley School for the Blind), as well as the video *Birth Order* (Learning Seed, 1992).

Kevin holds the CSP designation (Certified Speaking Professional), which is the highest earned honor in the speaking profession. Fewer than five hundred people in the world hold that honor for speaking excellence. Kevin is married, has two children, and lives in suburban Chicago. Contact Kevin at kevin@kevinoc.com or via www.kevinoc.com.

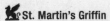